"At some point in our life, our faith is tested. It can feel like God is hidden and out of reach. We wonder if we can count on God's presence. *When Faith Feels Fragile* teaches us how to recognize the many ways that God touches us in the course of our daily routine. Drawing on the practical wisdom of life experience, Father Scott Hurd explores the deeper spiritual meaning by finding parallels in Scripture and Christian spirituality. We learn how to 'open ourselves up to the gift of faith and hold it close to our hearts.'"

— His Eminence Cardinal Donald Wuerl,
Archbishop of Washington

"I love Father Hurd's style—good-humored and inviting, brimming with the wisdom of Sacred Scripture and the saints, and rich in practical advice. Don't just get this book for the 'wary, weak, and wandering' cradle Catholics in your life—get it for the new converts, to help them keep the flame of faith alive."

— Dawn Eden, author of *The Thrill of the Chaste*

"If there's one thing we all feel with frequency, it's our fragility. And if there's one gift we need to share more generously, it's our faith. In forty accessible and easy to read chapters, Father Scott Hurd offers deep insight and practical tasks so that we can move forward in peace, healed by the gift of faith. If life has you anxious, tired, and confused, each chapter is a sermon for strength. Father Hurd relies on his wealth of personal and pastoral experience to provide a reader—possessing even but a spark of belief—with some welcome medicine for the soul."

— Father Robert P. Reed, President,
The CatholicTV Network

"When faith becomes a fragile thing, it usually means we are feeling challenged on many fronts and are worn down. With *When Faith Feels Fragile,* Father Scott Hurd takes a respectful look at the soul when it has come to feel incapable of bearing very much, and reminds us that, in order to regain strength, we must at least take on the little tasks that both nourish the spirit and help it to grow some muscle. In short, sometimes humorous, always insightful chapters, *When Faith Feels Fragile* goes down like a strengthening broth meant to restore mind, soul, and spirit. It is a very good recipe for when the appetite of faith has been waning."

— Elizabeth Scalia, author of
*Strange Gods: Unmasking the Idols in Everyday Life*

# When Faith Feels
# FRAGILE

# When Faith Feels
# FRAGILE

## Help for the Wary, Weak, and Wandering

R. Scott Hurd

**auline**
BOOKS & MEDIA

Boston

Library of Congress Cataloging-in-Publication Data

Hurd, R. Scott.
  When faith feels fragile : help for the wary, weak, and wandering / R. Scott
Hurd.
     pages cm
  ISBN-13: 978-0-8198-8343-8
  ISBN-10: 0-8198-8343-3
  1.  Spiritual life--Catholic Church. 2.  Faith development. 3.  Spiritual
formation--Catholic Church.  I. Title.
  BX2350.2.H79 2013
  248.4'82--dc23

                              2013019913

Cover design by Rosana Usselmann

Cover photo: istockphoto.com

"P" and PAULINE are registered trademarks of the Daughters of St. Paul.

Published by Pauline Books & Media, 50 Saint Pauls Avenue, Boston, MA 02130-3491

Printed in the U.S.A.

www.pauline.org

Pauline Books & Media is the publishing house of the Daughters of St. Paul, an international congregation of women religious serving the Church with the communications media.

1 2 3 4 5 6 7 8 9                                    17 16 15 14 13

*To my three wonderful kids:*
*Charlie, Winnie, and Isabel.*
*May God always bless you and keep you strong in faith.*

# Contents

Part 2

# CHURCHY THINGS TO DO

Part 3

## PRACTICAL THINGS TO DO

Part 4

FUN THINGS TO DO

# Part 1

# *All About Faith*

 CHAPTER 1

# Take the Offer

The crowd was eager with expectation. Many had traveled from around the globe to be renewed and encouraged in their faith, and they hoped that their prominent speaker wouldn't disappoint. But what they heard must have come as something of a surprise. "Our faith is weak," the speaker confessed, "our faith is shaky."[1]

These words weren't intended as a criticism or a put-down. Instead, they were meant to acknowledge and confirm what many in that crowd were likely thinking, or even fearing, to assure them that it was okay if their faith felt fragile, and that they weren't alone.

The speaker that day was no less than Cardinal Timothy Dolan, the Catholic Archbishop of New York, and his audience happened to be three hundred and fifty of the nearly two million young people who converged on Madrid, Spain, for

World Youth Day in 2011. But Dolan's words could have been meant for anyone. Perhaps they resonate with you.

Feeling that our faith is fragile is not necessarily a bad thing. In fact, to accept our faith's weakness is a good step toward our faith becoming stronger. Even Mother Teresa struggled with her faith. In a letter to a friend, during a dark and difficult moment, she could admit: "I have no faith. I don't believe."[2] If Mother Teresa wasn't exempt from such feelings, we probably won't be either. Yet Mother Teresa is now well on her way to being declared a saint. This can give us great encouragement that there's hope for our faith too.

If your faith feels fragile, don't despair. It happens to just about everyone at some point, for any number of reasons. More often than not, it springs from a combination of factors.

First, there's all the "cultural static" we have to contend with. The world shouts at us, "Look at me! Buy me! Sleep with me!" and we can't seem to hear anything else—especially God, who typically speaks in whispers. Information overload from every conceivable form of media makes us hesitant to add other voices to the mix, including God's, which gets drowned out. Responsibilities with work, family, and other day-to-day activities distract and exhaust us so much that making time for matters of faith seems like a luxury, or something to put off for a day when we're less stressed. We don't intend to push God away; he simply drops off the radar screen. And when he's out of sight, he's out of mind.

Perhaps our faith feels fragile because it hasn't been fed. We're not entirely starving, but we're malnourished. Our formal religious education might have ended years ago, and it may have been very good. But even so, it was likely intended for kids, and it hasn't always prepared us to face the ups and down of adulthood. We seek guidance on how our faith might impact relationships, work, parenting, finances, our losses and hurts. At times, we may have found ourselves turning to self-help books, talk shows, the gym, or therapists to find answers, and we wonder where our faith factors in.

Pain can weaken faith too. Without exception, life beats us up. Hearts get broken; dreams are shattered. Relationships and parenting are a struggle, as is keeping bread on the table. Growing older can be painful, scary, and lonely. Dear ones die, leaving an empty space only they can fill. We experience such things, or see their impact on those close to us, and our faith's foundations can get shaken.

It could be that Church members haven't exactly manifested the love of Christ to us. Upon learning that I'm a priest, one woman's words to me were: "Are you judgmental?" I was a bit taken aback at the time but came to appreciate that judgmentalism is what she'd come to expect from clergy. She's not alone. Many have experienced Church as hypocritical, cold, uncaring, untrustworthy, boring, or more concerned with money or rules than with matters of the Spirit. The sad fact is that a number of good people today prefer to describe themselves as "spiritual" rather than "religious" because they've found organized religion to be a turnoff.

We probably know people who've stopped going to Mass altogether, and from all outward appearances they seem to be doing just fine. Perhaps we've seen a billboard at Christmastime proclaiming something like, "Why believe in God? Just be good for goodness' sake!" and it made us pause for a moment. But at the end of the day, that's not for us. Our faith may feel fragile, but it's still important to us. Deep inside we know that something vital and precious would be lost if we let go of our faith. We want to have faith. At the very least, we want to want to have faith!

And let's face it: it's not always easy to have faith. After all, it requires us to believe in a God we can't even see. God so often seems to hide himself that we can wonder if there's even a God who's hiding. We can sympathize with the young woman who, when completing the "religion" section of her social media profile, wrote: "Unsure, but willing to entertain offers."

The good news is God has an offer to make. He's holding out his hand to us even now. Faith does require action on our part, to be sure. But at the end of the day, faith is God's gift. We just have to take it.

This book is about accepting God's offer of faith. Together we'll explore what faith is and consider ways we can open ourselves to this gift and hold it close to our hearts. It will take effort, that's for certain. But then that's true of anything worthwhile. As we make that effort, we might offer an honest prayer: "I believe; help my unbelief!" (Mk 9:24 *RSV*). That's a prayer from the Bible, by the way. And it's one that God is more than happy to answer.

 CHAPTER 2

# Get Some R and R

While sitting in my room at a resort hotel, flipping through the hotel chain's promotional magazine, I was struck by the language used to describe what was offered at their establishments. Words like *healing, harmony, purification, wholeness, peace, renewal, bliss,* and *nourishment* jumped off the page at me. It was even claimed that my spirit would be *inspired* and my soul would be *warmed.*

After reading the magazine, I started seeing this language everywhere. The hotel bathroom's dry skin cream was "renewing body lotion." The complimentary needle and thread was a "restoring kit." The tag on the bottled water encouraged me to "make my body happy." And the café downstairs promised that their coffee would "rejuvenate (my) spirit and refresh (my) outlook"—which is a lot of pressure to put on a cup of coffee!

Maybe this is just marketing jargon used around resorts and spas. Or perhaps all the talk about healing, restoration, wholeness, happiness, and peace is a reflection of a very real longing we all have: a longing not just for a little rest and relaxation but for something deeper, something that strikes at the very center of who we are as human beings—a longing to be healed of our wounds, to have our brokenness made whole, to discover lasting peace and abiding joy; a longing for something we were made for but somehow lost.

Such longings can't be satisfied by a visit to a resort, as nice as that might be. Only Jesus can provide us with the rest and refreshment we seek, as he himself says: "Come to me, all you grown weary and burdened, and I will *refresh* you. Take my yoke upon you and learn from me, for I am gentle and humble hearted, and you will find *rest* for your souls; for my yoke is easy, and my burden light" (Mt 11:28–30, *Alba House*).

Jesus is speaking of the blessings we receive through living a life of faith in him. His words are comforting and soothing, to be sure. At the same time, they're also somewhat challenging because it's easier to associate rest and refreshment with resorts than it is with a "yoke." When I think of a yoke, the first image that comes to mind is that of sweaty oxen laboring to pull a plow across a muddy field—not a very refreshing or restful picture! Therefore, we might ask: Just what does Jesus mean by his "yoke," and how can it be restful or refreshing?

To answer this question, we need to understand that most of the first-century men and women who first heard Jesus' words imagined God to be distant, unknowable, and impersonal, and had been taught that following him required keeping hundreds of very specific commandments called the "yoke of the Law." Keeping these cumbersome rules was a heavy burden to bear and must have been physically, emotionally, and spiritually exhausting.

Two thousand years later, things haven't changed too much. People still believe God to be distant, impersonal, or uncaring. Perhaps we ourselves think that way at times. Thankfully, Jesus' words can appeal to us just as much as they inspired people back then. You see, the yoke Jesus invites us to wear isn't a burdensome list of rules handed down by an inaccessible God. Instead, the yoke Jesus refers to is Jesus himself! Jesus invites us to yoke ourselves to him through a life of faith. By following and trusting him through all the twists and turns that life may throw at us, and by embracing his wisdom and teaching, we'll find the rest and refreshment that he promises and that we long for.

This doesn't mean that our life will become like an extended resort stay. When he spoke of rest and refreshment, Jesus didn't promise to take away our burdens. What he does do is help us carry them. By yoking ourselves to him, our burdens will become lighter because he'll help us bear the load. In a sense, Jesus has already taken the load from us. On the cross he took upon himself all of the suffering and agony of a broken humanity that we all might be redeemed and healed. Today he invites us to add our burden to that load, so that it will be his strength, and not ours, that will bear it up.

Think of it this way: a yoke joins a pair of oxen together and makes them a team. When our lives are yoked with Jesus in faith, we're teamed with him. He'll pull our load alongside us, giving us strength and courage to carry on when we might otherwise feel like giving up. He'll give our lives direction and purpose, steering us in the right direction when we, if left on our own, wouldn't know if we should turn to the right or to the left. He'll teach us along the way as well, helping us to see our lives and our world as he sees them, and revealing God's hand in situations in which we might not have seen it before. And Jesus will be our constant traveling companion, staying by our side in good times and bad, during seasons of sorrow and joy, and being our truest friend when life gets lonely and other friends just can't be found.

So what about resorts? Many lovely things might be found there, there's no doubt about that! But we could spend an entire lifetime, traveling from one exotic location to another, being pampered in every conceivable way, and still not find that rest and refreshment we're looking for in the depths of our souls. Only Jesus can offer that.

"Come here," resorts invite us, as they entice us with an illusion of the "good life." Jesus says to us instead, "Come to me," with the promise of a life that is truly good, and a rest, and a refreshment unlike anything this world is able to give. That's the gift, and the benefit, of faith.

## CHAPTER 3

# Tend Your Garden

When I moved into my home, I inherited a backyard that had once been landscaped and beautiful. Yet when I first saw it, everything was completely overgrown with weeds because it had hardly been touched for twenty years. "If you don't stay on top of it," the previous owner reflected, "nature quickly takes over." Ever since then, I've spent endless hours in my yard—weeding, tilling, mulching, seeding, planting, fertilizing, and weeding again. Yet as soon as I think I can take a break, "nature quickly takes over," and the crabgrass and dandelions make their appearance once again.

Jesus told a story of a farmer and his soil that reminds me of my backyard. When the farmer scattered his seed, he encountered different conditions of soil. Some was rocky, some was hard, some was choked with thorns and weeds, and some soil Jesus described as "good." Not surprisingly, only the good soil produced a healthy growth.

This story is about our life of faith. Jesus invites us to be like good soil so we can be blessed with a vibrant faith. But as with my backyard, we'll have to invest time and effort in order to enrich our soil and remove any rocks and weeds that might choke our faith's growth.

One way to enrich our soil is by clearing away the distracting clutter that can easily fill our minds and days, leaving space for little else. I'll never forget walking down a sidewalk on a summer's day, when about forty teenagers got off a tour bus and began advancing toward me. Without exception, each one of them was glued to a mobile device and was texting or posting or surfing or whatever—which is fine! The problem was that I had to jump out of their way to avoid being trampled because they were completely oblivious to what was going on around them.

And isn't that what too much electronic media can do to any one of us, including those of us well past our teenage years? We can get so sucked into the Web, social media, blogging, texting, shopping, playing games, downloading stuff, and even watching good old-fashioned TV, that we risk ignoring more essential things, including our life of faith. Just like the phalanx of distracted teenagers who failed to see me approaching them, we can get so distracted that we can miss Jesus, even if he passes right by us.

Of course, it's not just electronic media that can distract us. It's so easy, in our culture, to become overscheduled. Our lives get stuffed full of activity; we speak of being busy "24/7." Some of these activities are necessary or unavoidable, to be sure. However, it's easy to fill our lives with busyness for other reasons—to avoid dealing with problems we don't want to face, to compete against others in the rat race, or because we're searching for purpose, meaning, or a sense of self-worth through our accomplishments. Many of us struggle with workaholism—a particularly sinister addiction because it's so often perceived to be a virtue. The end result of all this is that we're left with little time or energy for the things of God. Our soil becomes poor; "nature quickly takes over."

What is it that might keep us from spending more time on matters of faith? Our exercise routine? Social media? A hobby? Friendships? Unnecessary overtime? Volunteering? A special project? Statistics show that we Americans are hard workers. But other statistics show that many of us make poor use of the leisure time we have. For instance, the typical American, both kids and adults, watches twenty-eight hours of TV a week. Video gamers, again both kids and adults, play video games an average of ten hours a week. Golfers, runners, and other sports enthusiasts can spend equally as much time on their passions.

Might we not spend some of our time differently? Would it be possible to devote more of it to getting to know our Lord? We appreciate that people need to spend time with each other in order to truly know each other. That's true for spouses, friends, family, or workmates. It's also true when it comes to us and our Lord.

Think of it this way: to most of those who encountered him, Jesus was simply a distant acquaintance. They knew of him, perhaps even knew a little bit about him, but not enough to really know who he was. Certainly not enough to love him! It was only those who traveled with him, ate with him, and listened to his teaching who truly came to understand who he was and appreciate how much he loved them. They had made the time to get to know him.

To give a gift of time is to give a part of our lives we can't replace. Time is a finite resource; once it's gone, it's gone. To give time, therefore, is a sacrifice. But sacrifice, of course, is the essence of love. That's why time is a gift that Jesus longs for us to give him. To do this, one bishop invites the young people he confirms to remember two numbers: 144 and 168. The number 144 is the number of ten-minute periods in the day, and 168 is the number of hours in the week. He then challenges the young people to give ten minutes of each day for prayer or the study of God's Word and one hour a week to attend Sunday Mass.[1] That's a solid foundation for any of us to start strengthening our life of faith; it's a good beginning to tending our garden, enriching our soil, and keeping the weeds and crabgrass at bay.

We're all busy people, there's no doubt about that! Our time is precious, as it should be. But to cultivate our life of faith, that it might become a beautiful garden, our precious Lord invites us to spend more of that precious time—with him.

 CHAPTER 4

# Take Baby Steps

Society today is incredibly fast-paced. Activities that might once have taken hours, days, weeks, or even months can now be done almost instantaneously. With the Internet, old-fashioned letters are disparaged as "snail mail." Vast information is placed at our fingertips, eliminating trips to the library. Banking and shopping can be done online. For news, we don't need to wait for the morning paper because the news is broadcast continuously on cable television. Microwaves heat our prepared meals in minutes. We're surrounded by timesaving technology! And for the most part, it's wonderfully beneficial. The down side, however, is that it can make us impatient because we so seldom have to wait for anything anymore.

Our impatience can even impact our life of faith. We look for something that will change us overnight—a retreat, a book, a spiritual experience—anything! We hope for a quick fix. Perhaps we're familiar with the story of Saint Paul, as told in Scripture. While on his way to Damascus to persecute Christians, the risen Jesus appeared to him and reversed the course of his life. Tradition even speaks of Saint Paul falling off his horse at this encounter, which the Church commemorates each year as the "Conversion of Saint Paul." We might think, "If Saint Paul's life could be dramatically changed like that, why can't mine? All I need is for Jesus to appear and knock me out of my saddle!"

This "Conversion of Saint Paul," however, was in reality only the beginning of his conversion. He had just been introduced to Jesus for the first time; his faith journey as a Christian had commenced but was far from being completed. Over the following years, Saint Paul wrote of his continuing growth in faith, and he frequently described it as a struggle. In his letters, he speaks of fighting the good fight, running the race, beating his body, engaging in battle with the armor of God, and pressing on toward a prize he had yet to reach—a prize, he insisted, that could not be gained this side of heaven. Until then, he had to keep putting one foot in front of the other. His faith journey would take an entire lifetime. So will ours.

Perhaps, as with Saint Paul, God broke into our life in a dramatic fashion. Maybe it's happened more than once. Hopefully this has had a powerful and positive impact on us. That was certainly God's intention! Nevertheless, these "mountaintop experiences" are but highlights in a lifelong discipleship that will require discipline, patience, and perseverance. As hard as we might try, there's no being transformed from Homer Simpson to Mother Teresa overnight.

Nevertheless, there's often a part of us that hopes we might. For Catholics, this is especially true during the season of Lent, those forty days each year when we make a special effort to grow in faith. According to a priest friend of mine, Lent is our "season of great expectations" because we often hope to achieve too much. In our quest for overnight sainthood, we take on a Lenten discipline that's way too demanding—you know, we're going to "give up" this, that, and the other; we're going to fast, pray the rosary, and go to Mass every day, *et cetera*. We might even manage to keep this up for a while, but then we burn out and get discouraged. We get "spiritual indigestion" because we've bitten off more than we can chew.

In our journey of faith, we often must be satisfied with baby steps instead of giant leaps; we need to measure our progress by the inch not the mile. And this requires patience. Sometimes it might seem like we're not making any headway at all, or that we're even sliding backward. We can be tempted to give up and think that we're never going to grow. But we need to remember three things: First, although we might want to give up on ourselves, God never gives up on us. Second, God never wants us to get discouraged because he doesn't want us to lose hope, since life without hope is hell on earth! Third, God is more patient with us than we are with ourselves. He often stretches us very slowly because he doesn't want us to snap and break.

It's easy to underestimate God's patience. Since we're often impatient, we assume that God must be too. Surely, we're tempted to think, God must have a line drawn in the sand somewhere, a straw that will break the proverbial camel's back. Thankfully, he doesn't. Julian of Norwich, a great Catholic woman of the Middle Ages, described God as being "in His house, filling it with joy and mirth . . . with a marvelous melody of endless love,"[1]—a picture quite different from the stern and impatient figure that we sometimes imagine God to be. He is eternal, after all. He has all the time in the world!

And it's a good thing, too, because God knows we need plenty of time to become the saints he created us to be. One account of Jesus' healing a blind man suggests this to us. After Jesus touched his eyes a first time, the man could see, but his vision was blurry; people looked like "walking trees." It was only after Jesus touched him a second time that his sight was fully restored. Had Jesus' first attempt failed? Did he need a "do over?" Not at all. Instead, this story reminds us that, in our faith lives, there is no quick fix. To see the way Jesus wanted him to see, Jesus had to touch the blind man twice. For us to see the way Jesus wants us to see, he'll need to touch us many, many more times than that.

Yet that shouldn't worry us. God is patient with us, and he asks us to be patient too. Rome wasn't built in a day, and neither are God's saints! Three thousand years later, Rome is still under construction. And, "pardon our dust," so are we. But that's okay. Jesus is a carpenter. He knows how to finish the job.

 Chapter 5

# Don't Get Off the Bus

At a Christmas party, a friend approached me with tears in her eyes. Her father had died earlier in the year, and her faith was deeply shaken. "I'm not really sure what I believe any more," she said. She wondered if God even existed at all.

My friend's experience is not unusual. When a loved one dies, it can seem like God doesn't care, or that he's punishing us. We may, like my friend, even doubt that God is real.

Other things can lead us to doubt as well. We see wars, injustice, hatred, poverty, immorality, sickness, and disease, and we think: "Where is God in all of this? Surely a good God wouldn't allow all this pain!"

Our society's skepticism doesn't help either. Many around us dismiss religious faith as a weekend hobby—if they don't frown on it altogether. Critics insist that faith is dangerous because it's been used to justify bigotry and violence. Others maintain that faith is simply an evolutionary by-product no longer needed in our modern age. Only the ignorant or the needy, seeking an emotional crutch, still cling to faith.

Poor examples given by religious people, through their anger, self-righteousness, public indiscretions, love of wealth, or lack of compassion can also give rise to doubt. For him to believe in the Christian redeemer, insisted atheist philosopher Friedrich Nietzsche, "more like saved ones would his disciples have to appear unto me!"[1]

Sometimes we find it hard to accept what our faith calls us to believe. Certain things just don't seem to make sense or add up. I believe that it was the noted preacher, Father Walter Burghardt, who confessed that sometimes he'd lie in bed at night and wonder how the Christian faith made sense. Even the Lord's disciples wrestled with doubts. Once, after Jesus spoke of eating his flesh and drinking his blood, many stomped off in discouragement because they couldn't stomach his teaching. "This saying is hard," they complained. "Who can accept it?" Jesus asked his friends if they too were going to leave. "Master, to whom shall we go?" replied Peter. "You have the words of eternal life" (see Jn 6:60–68).

Peter's answer suggests that the disciples themselves struggled to accept that teaching. Later on they would come to embrace it, however, because instead of walking away, they continued to follow Jesus, even though as yet they didn't quite understand who he was or some of what he said. They may indeed have had doubts. But their doubts didn't lead to desertion, as they trusted—or at least hoped—that Jesus knew what he was talking about. That's a good example for us to follow.

The good news is that doubt isn't altogether a bad thing. When facing doubt, there's no need to panic. It's a temptation, to be sure, but it's also a test that God allows to strengthen our faith. Saint Thérèse of Lisieux sometimes wondered during a long and painful illness if God existed at all. Yet this experience ultimately deepened her faith. Like hers, our faith can be strengthened through doubt. In fact, periods of doubt might even be essential to growth in faith. Gordon Allport, an esteemed Harvard psychologist of religion, insisted that struggles with doubts are typically necessary if we're to enjoy a healthy faith.[2]

As we mature in faith, we typically shed images of God we inherited or formed as children. For instance, children may imagine God to be like a superhero, a fairy godmother, a truant officer, a grey-bearded old man—or even a combination of these! Which is fine. But a child's image of God cannot sustain an adult. Our understanding of God must mature as we mature. For this to happen, we may encounter periods of doubt. We'll wonder, "Is God really like I've imagined him to be?" Perhaps not. But that's okay. At times like this, we may think we're doubting the existence of God, while what we're really doubting is a false conception of God. The experience may be difficult, even painful. But at the end of the day it's essential.

The story is told of a student who returned home after her first semester away at college. She was distressed and went to see her parish priest straightaway. "Father," she cried, "I've lost my faith!" Without missing a beat, her priest replied, "Good! Now we can replace it with something better." She had expected him to respond with disappointment and worry. How shocked she was that the priest was pleased! But he knew that she had to first "lose" her faith—the faith of her childhood—in order to embrace the faith of an adult. That was the experience of Dostoyevsky, the great Russian writer. "It is not as a child that

I believe and confess Jesus Christ," he explained. "My 'hosanna' is born of a furnace of doubt."[3]

While in the "furnace of doubt," however, it's critical that we maintain the practice of our faith. We need to persist while puzzled and continue when confused. That may seem hypocritical, but it's not. It's much easier to resolve our faith doubts while going through the motions than it is if we've stopped moving altogether. Keep praying even if you're not sure anyone is listening. We can maintain our faith simply by making acts of faith. At times like this, we would do well to take the advice of Reverend Austin Farrer, a dear friend of C. S. Lewis: "Attend the Mass well, make a good Communion, pray for the grace you need, and you will know that you are not dealing with the empty air."[4]

The life of faith is a journey. We don't always know where we're headed; the road ahead may look dark; we may find ourselves without map and compass; doubts arise and we may fear that the whole trip is pointless. If we think that way, we won't be the first. Take a deep breath, and keep moving on. It's like a priest friend of mine once said: "We may wonder if we're headed to the right stop. Just don't get off the bus!"

 CHAPTER 6

# Make the Choice

In B. J. Thomas's 1968 classic *Hooked on a Feeling*, the singer believes that he's loved because he can feel it.[1] Anyone who's ever fallen in love can understand that sentiment. Being in love feels wonderful; it's how every romance gets its start.

Yet the initial experience of feeling "in love" is never permanent. It's great while it lasts and is usually necessary to bring two people together in the first place. But it's just as necessary for that feeling to fade away at some point in order for the relationship to grow and mature.

The problem is we sometimes want the feeling of being in love to last forever because there's nothing else quite like it. That's why, when the feeling vanishes, we may fear that our relationship is in trouble or even about to end. As the singer in another old hit song lamented, when we've lost that "lovin' feelin,'" a relationship is as good as "gone, gone, gone."[2]

Love can indeed give rise to wonderful feelings. It's a mistake, however, to equate love *with* those feelings. As a matter of fact, true love can exist without any good feelings. Consider the sacrifice of Jesus, which is history's greatest act of love. To put it terribly mildly, the crucifixion didn't feel good at all.

The absence of good feelings does not indicate the absence of love. This is true for our relationships with other people, and it's true of our relationship with God. On occasion, especially when we've just come to faith, we may feel very much in love with God and that God is very much in love with us. We can feel like a newlywed, which is not surprising given that the Bible often compares our relationship with God to that of a bride and a bridegroom.

At times like this, prayer is easy and makes us feel warm and inspired. Worship is exciting and uplifting. We may be blessed with powerful and moving spiritual experiences. We can be grateful to God for whenever he touches our lives in these ways. He does this to remind us that he's near and to assure us of his love.

At other times, however, we may not feel close to God at all. Prayer is hard and uninspiring. Worship seems dull and routine. Spiritual experiences dry up. No longer do we feel in love with God or that God loves us. We may worry that we've done something wrong, that God has forgotten us, or that he's stopped caring. We may even wonder if there's a God to "feel" at all.

It's tempting to think this way when God has felt close to us in the past but seems absent to us now. However, to *feel* that God is absent doesn't mean that he *is* absent. In fact, the lack of feelings may actually be a good sign that our relationship with him is growing deeper, instead of splitting apart.

When our friendship is new, God may well use our feelings to draw us closer to him. He does this to "lure us in," so to speak. If he didn't, we might not be attracted to him in the first place. However, God may later withdraw those good feelings, not to punish us, but to strengthen us. He does this because he doesn't want us to get "hooked on a feeling" with him; he wants our relationship to be based on much more than that. He wants us to love him, but not just because he makes us feel good. That's why he sometimes withdraws the good feelings. The goal is for us to love God, not the feelings God gives.

Relationships based on feelings can become selfish because they're dependent on the feelings one enjoys. But true love isn't selfish. Instead, true love is self-less; it's more focused on giving than it is on receiving. The love God offers to us, and the love he invites us to share in return, is a commitment and a choice. This love loves when it doesn't feel like loving; it does what it does, not just because it might feel good, but because it's the right thing to do. Sacrifice is at the heart of this love—as Jesus has shown us on the cross.

Faith is easy when we feel good; faith is hard when we feel nothing. Faith based on feelings is fragile; faith without feelings is ultimately stronger. God wants our faith to be strong; that's why he withdraws the feelings. When this happens, there's no cause for alarm. Our faith is being tested so it can grow. It can be tempting, however, to try to recreate or rediscover the feelings we once had. But that approach will only leave us frustrated. The best thing to do is persevere by continuing to pray, worship, and serve, in spite of any absence of good spiritual feelings. Woody Allen famously said that fifty percent of life is simply showing up. The same might be said of our life of faith: a great deal of it is just "showing up" by keeping on keeping on.

Think of it this way: just because a honeymoon is over doesn't mean that a marriage is over. Far from it! The honeymoon is only the beginning. That's true for husbands and wives, and it's true of our relationship with God. Hopefully, we'll look back on the honeymoon with fondness and gratitude. It wasn't the end of the good times, to be sure. But we'll also recall the rough times when happy feelings seemed like a distant memory. That's when we hung on to the commitment we made, to stick together for better and for worse, for richer and for poorer, in sickness and in health, in good times and in bad. Loving feelings weren't what got us through. It was our loving choices. In hindsight, we'll know that they brought us closer and made us stronger. And we'll realize that it was all part of a plan.

CHAPTER 7

# Follow Like Sheep

A Texas cattle rancher once said to me, "Father, there's a reason why Jesus didn't say, 'I am the good cowboy.'" Cows, he explained, are stubborn creatures. To get them going in the right direction, they need to be prodded from behind. Sheep, on the other hand, happily follow their shepherd. That's why Jesus called himself a good shepherd. He wants us to be like sheep and follow him. Often, however, we act more like cows. We'd prefer to take the lead.

This was evident in a debate between two best-selling authors: Rick Warren, a Christian, and Sam Harris, an atheist. At one point, Harris spoke glowingly about the benefits of spirituality, meditation, love, and feeling connected to the cosmos. Warren challenged him, however, and insisted that while Harris might indeed be a spiritual person, he resisted the idea of God being in control—of God being "in the driver's seat."[1]

Even we who believe in God can resist letting him sit in our driver's seat. Americans especially: we value independence and self-reliance; it's part of our pioneering heritage. We teach our children to "believe in themselves" because we want them to grow into confident adults. That's fine, until children conclude that they're to believe *only* in themselves. "Father," a young girl once asked me, "who should I believe in more: God or myself?" "Definitely God," I insisted, "because we can fool ourselves." She paused, thanked me, and quietly walked away. She was less than convinced.

She's also not alone. We may fear that to trust God is to risk losing our identity. After all, aren't we told to "follow your dreams" and "be yourself"? Yes! As Saint Francis de Sales said, "Be yourself, and be that well!" But to truly "be yourself" is to be the person God created you to be; to "follow your dreams" is to follow the footsteps of Jesus, in whom all our deepest hopes and aspirations are fulfilled. For this to happen, we need to let God call the shots. This is known as "surrender." Doing it won't wipe out our identity. It will just wipe out our selfishness.

"Surrender" can sound scary; it's what's done when we're beaten by enemies who take away our freedom. But God is no enemy; he's no threat to our freedom. Quite the opposite: God wants us to be free—free to do what's right, free to do what will bring us true peace and lasting happiness, free to be who we were created to be.

We have a standing invitation from God to surrender our lives to him. However, we typically surrender to God only when there seem to be no other alternatives. We often wait until we've been brought *to* our knees before we're willing to get *on* our knees, because it's at times like that when God's call to surrender is heard the loudest. That call, nevertheless, is always there.

But how do we accept that invitation? Take the first three steps of any Twelve Step program: First, acknowledge that there are things in our lives over which we have no control; second, believe in God who loves us and wants to help us; and third, turn our lives over to God.

Surrendering to God involves handing over our plans. "If you want to make God laugh," wrote Saint Teresa of Avila, "tell him your plans!" God laughs whenever we make our plans without him and then expect him to accept our decisions, bless them, and bring them success. That's putting the cart before the horse. As Christians, we should first consider what God's plans might be and then pray for the grace to carry them out.

Certainly God is concerned about our "big" plans: those about family, job, education, home, relationships, major purchases, volunteer commitments, and medical procedures. But does God care if we order a pizza? Absolutely! Think of it this way: would pizza be a treat or another unhealthy lifestyle choice? Would we be supporting a local restaurant that creates jobs, or letting good leftovers spoil? Is pizza in our budget? Or are we breaking the bank? As Christians, it's good to ask questions like these all the time. They help God help us to keep our lives going in the right direction.

Surrendering involves making God's plans our own. And that can be tricky. God's will isn't always clear. Sometimes we'll be unsure or confused; sometimes we'll make mistakes. But that's okay. Just wanting to do God's will is pleasing to him. If we take a wrong turn, he'll always be there to get us back on track. As the old saying goes, God can write straight with crooked lines! God doesn't demand success as the world understands it; he simply asks us to do our best and have faith in him. Not faith in a particular outcome, mind you, but faith that he loves us, keeps his promises, and always knows what's best.

To surrender is a daily decision, as a friend of mine once stressed in a homily. He stood before an altar with a big bag stuffed with paper, held it up, and said, "This is our life. As Christians we seek to give our lives to Christ." To demonstrate this, he turned around and reverently placed the bag before the altar. "But then," he said, "we always try to take our life back again," and he unceremoniously snatched the bag up. The point was that while we may have good intentions to surrender our lives to God, we invariably hold or take something back. That's why we need to surrender ourselves over and over again.

With time, however, we'll find that the more we surrender, the less we'll worry. The more we turn our lives over to God, the more our faith will grow as we'll come to experience that God is worthy of our trust. And the more we trust, the easier it is to surrender and follow like a sheep. No longer will God be laughing at our plans. He'll be smiling because we've embraced his.

## CHAPTER 8

# Don't Look Down!

A dear friend of mine has truly endured a "hard knock life." Over the years, she's had far more than her fair share of marital, parental, financial, physical, and psychological woes. Yet when living through her many challenges and difficulties, she's learned to keep sight of the fact that Jesus is always with her—even during her darkest, most difficult days.

My friend speaks of faith in terms of her relationship with her dad, with whom she was very close. For instance, when teaching her to ride a bike, he would say, "Keep looking at me! Keep your eyes on me! If you look down, you're going to wobble and fall!" And when he taught her to swim, he'd open wide his arms and say, "Don't be afraid and don't look around—just swim to me!"

These fond memories remind my friend that faith involves keeping one's eyes on Jesus, especially when one is anxious, afraid, or when the going gets rough. She explains that so often when we find ourselves in trouble, we think we need to cry out to God and bring our distress to his attention. But in reality, Jesus is always there with us. We just need to be able to see him, with eyes of faith.

Saint Peter once learned the importance of keeping his eyes on Jesus when he and his friends found themselves in the midst of a storm (see Mt 14:22–33). The wind was howling, the waves were pounding, and their little boat was being dangerously tossed about. And then, from seemingly out of nowhere, Jesus appeared. He didn't immediately calm the storm. Instead, he came to his friends in the *midst* of the storm in order to help them learn about faith.

While he walked on the water, Jesus invited Peter to come to him, and what happened next is very instructive for us. As long as Peter kept his eyes focused on Jesus, he wasn't overwhelmed by the wind and the waves. Instead, he was able to rise above them! It was only when he took his eyes off Jesus that he began to sink and be filled with fear.

When we find ourselves being tossed about by the storms of life, we can take a cue from Peter. As long as we keep our eyes on Jesus, by trying our best to stay close to him in faith and trust, we won't drown, sink into despair, or be paralyzed by fear. "Those who keep faith in Jesus," wrote Saint Augustine, "can walk upon the waves of the storms of life." Why? Because we will hear Jesus saying to us, as he said to Peter: "Take courage, it is I; do not be afraid" (Mt 14:27).

Jesus wishes to fill us with courage when we're confronted with frightening or painful situations. But that's not all. He wants to use them to help us grow in faith. He's not punishing us. Instead, he invites us to view them as an opportunity. At times, we may be confused or angry that he has allowed something to happen to us. Yet Jesus asks us to trust that he can always bring good out of evil and use even the worst circumstances to shape us into more loving people, and make us a bit more like him.

According to Scripture, Jesus "learned obedience from what he suffered" (Heb 5:8). We can learn that too, when we suffer, by surrendering our plans to God. We can also learn to trust more in God than in ourselves, because when we suffer, we typically can't rely on our own resources. Also, suffering can remind us that this life isn't all there is but that God has something better and more permanent in store for us. And we can learn humility as well, because painful situations often involve our having to swallow some pride.

Most importantly, through suffering we can learn how to love. We might even say that suffering is the "core curriculum" in the school of love. We suffer, wrote Pope Benedict XVI, "in order to become a person who truly loves."[1] In fact, to love is to suffer, he went on to explain, because love involves sacrifice, patience, forgiveness, and the risk of opening up and sharing ourselves with others who may hurt or reject us. Through this love, we can grow in compassion for others who may be suffering. And we can come to appreciate more fully the depths of Jesus' love for us.

We've been told that God is love. At the same time, we know that everyone suffers; it's part of the human condition. But in a suffering world, it would be hard to accept that God is love if he were aloof or removed from all the suffering. If he were, it would be easy to write him off as uncaring or indifferent. But love is never indifferent. True love is always concerned; true love is always involved.

In a most powerful way, Jesus showed us, when he stretched out his arms upon a cross, that God is love. As God's Son, Jesus wasn't content to simply *tell* us of God's love. Instead, he wished to *show* us God's love. Even more, he wishes for us to *experience* that love, so that it's made real for us. And one way we can do that is to suffer like Jesus did. When we suffer like he suffered, we can come to say, "Now I understand! Now I know how much God loves me."

The last thing Jesus wants is for suffering to crush our faith. He'll allow it to challenge our faith, but only so that he can strengthen it. When Jesus came to Peter in the midst of the storm, he said to him, "Don't look down—look at me!" In the midst of our storms, Jesus says the same thing to us and invites us to look at him upon the cross. So we know that we're not alone. And so we know how deeply we're loved.

 CHAPTER 9

# Change Your Prescription

While registering for a 5k running race at a local community center, I noticed that one of my parishioners—someone I know rather well—was one of the race volunteers. I went over and started speaking with him. He was acting a little strangely until suddenly his eyes widened and he said, "Oh! You're Father Hurd! I didn't recognize you!" You see, I was dressed in running gear and a baseball cap, not my black clerical clothes, and we weren't in a church. My parishioner didn't expect to see me in the running context, looking the way I did. He wasn't even able to recognize me, although I was standing right in front of him.

We can do the very same thing when it comes to Jesus. It's easy to assume that we'll meet him only when we're doing typically "religious" activities: when we pray, read Scripture, go to Mass, and things like that. And obviously, we can and do meet Jesus in these ways! Yet it's just as possible to encounter him in other places and other contexts—in situations where we might not expect to find him, like the humdrum of our daily routine, at the office, when spending time with our family, on a stroll through our neighborhood, in the midst of our challenges, and in the faces of the needy and the poor. Indeed, Jesus is present in every situation in our lives. We simply have to open our eyes and look for him. To do this, we might say that we need to change our prescription!

At a retreat I attended years ago, the speaker put on a pair of cheap sunglasses that had white crosses painted on the lenses. He did this to demonstrate that as Christians, we should strive to see Jesus in all things and in all circumstances. It was a corny gesture, to be sure, but it has remained with me because its lesson is so true. To grow in faith, and to strengthen our faith when it feels weak, we can ask and try to discover Jesus where we haven't thought we'd encounter him before. Doing so is well worth the effort. As Thomas à Kempis wrote five hundred years ago: "If, however, you seek Jesus in all things, you will surely find him."[1]

To seek Jesus in all things, we might take a cue from two of Jesus's earliest disciples. They once failed to recognize Jesus, even though he was walking right alongside them and speaking to them (see Lk 24:13–35). It was only after they welcomed Jesus to spend the evening with them as a dinner guest that they were able to appreciate his presence with them. "Do what they did in order to recognize the Lord," wrote Saint Augustine. "They showed him hospitality."[2] In other words, should we welcome Jesus as a guest into every part of our lives, we will discover that he's all around us, all the time.

We can welcome Jesus more completely into our lives by welcoming him more into our minds. It's easy for our minds to become so distracted, preoccupied, or cluttered that thoughts of God or the things of God get squeezed out. I was reminded of this one morning as I walked my dog. When I left the house, my mind was filled with worries about the day's activities. As I walked, I looked only at the sidewalk. But then I caught myself, paused, and took in what was around me. A thin crescent moon was hanging in the clear cloudless sky, dew sparkled on the green grass as the sun appeared over the horizon, and a reverent silence was broken only by the lovely song of a distant bird. I couldn't help but offer a prayer of gratitude for this glimpse of God's glory that I surely would have missed had I kept my head down and my mind preoccupied.

As happened with me, God can be so absent from our thoughts that he can slip right past us without our even knowing it. That's why, in one of his letters, Saint Paul recommends that we change the way we think. He encourages us to fill our minds with thoughts of all that is true, honorable, just, pure, lovely, gracious, and excellent (see Phil 4:8). Saint Paul knew that when we lose sight of such things, our view of the world can become warped. We may see only the darkness and be blinded to the light. However, when we make an intentional effort to think about those things Saint Paul mentioned, we're reminded of what's good and beautiful in our world, all of which come from God's loving hand. And whenever we remember the good things of God, we become more aware of his presence all around us, and our faith becomes that much stronger.

Changing the way we think will also change our expectations. It may be that we don't expect to encounter God in many areas of our lives. We're a bit like the Bethlehem shepherd who gloomily told his wife as he left for work on the first Christmas

Eve, "*Nothing* ever happens on this job!" However, when we make the effort to look for God in more things, we'll begin to encounter him in more things, and our expectations will rise as a result.

Saint Teresa of Avila once reminded her fellow nuns that "The Lord walks among the pots and pans!"[3] In other words, we can look for God in the kitchen and shouldn't be surprised to meet him there. Indeed, the whole world is filled with the presence of God. It is his world, after all! Every situation we face, and every person we encounter, has the potential to be an encounter with God. Should we begin to open our eyes, this is what we'll come to expect. Blessed Charles de Foucauld put it well: Faith unmasks the world and reveals that God is in all things.[4]

## CHAPTER 10

# Eat Some Pie

One dreaded job interview question is: "What's your greatest weakness?" Because it's so feared it's often not answered entirely truthfully. Either the one answering will offer something bogus, such as "I work too hard," or attempt to present as a weakness something that's really a strength, like "I used to procrastinate, but now I'm more disciplined." At best, one might reveal a minor character flaw just to prove that he or she's not an egomaniac.

We typically hesitate to share our weaknesses, be it to a potential boss or anyone else. Sometimes we don't wish to admit them even to ourselves. We fear being rejected, ridiculed, exploited, put down, or taken advantage of. And so we put on masks to disguise our weaknesses and hide those parts of ourselves from the light of day.

Because our culture prizes power and influence, weaknesses are viewed strictly as liabilities. In our hypercompetitive world, it's feared that weaknesses can prevent us from successfully swimming with the sharks; they serve no good purpose in this cutthroat, dog-eat-dog climate. The problem is that this climate can turn us into nervous wrecks! It can also warp our understanding of God.

The confusion arises when we assume that God would use his power in the same way the world around us uses power. For instance, we might expect God to crush his enemies, fix all the world's problems with a wave of his hand, or force people to do what he wants them to do, like bow down and worship or get their act together. But when that doesn't happen, we can become frustrated and confused, and our faith can get rattled. At other times, we may assume that because God is so powerful, God looks down upon us as unimportant. He's "up there," so to speak, and could care less about us insignificant peons "down here."

Yet the truth is that God doesn't look down upon us. Quite the opposite! Instead of *looking down* upon us, he *came down* to us. In Jesus, God came to be one with us and to share our humanity. Jesus came to us in weakness, not in power. Although he is almighty, he chose to become weak in order to share our weakness and then save us from the mess our weakness has made.

While this is good news, it can also confuse us at the same time. As Blessed Teresa of Calcutta said, "We can understand the majesty of God; it is very difficult to understand the humility of God."[1] We can be comfortable believing in God's power, but the idea of a humble, suffering God can be hard to swallow. That's why it can be such a challenge to our faith. If we had a choice, we probably wouldn't want to see Jesus on a cross. We'd rather see him on a throne! But that's for the end of time. Not now.

We struggle to accept that God embraced weakness because our world sees no value in weakness. But God didn't reject weakness; he embraced it. God invites us to embrace our own weaknesses, so that we might understand him more and grow in faith. Doing this is called "humility." And Jesus himself shows us the way: ". . . coming in human likeness; and found human in appearance, he humbled himself, becoming obedient to death, even death on a cross" (Phil 2:7–8).

Humility can be misunderstood, and for some has acquired something of a bad rap. We might confuse it with putting one's self down, thinking badly of ourselves, or how we feel when we've been humiliated. But true humility, properly speaking, is none of those things. The word itself finds its roots in *humus*, the Latin word for "earth." To be humble, then, is to be "down to earth." Humility is liberating: it means that we don't have to pretend that we're someone we aren't. When we're humble, we can accept who we are and, because of that, we can accept that we have a need for God—a God who became weak—because at many times and in many ways we too are weak.

Embracing our weakness is a key to cultivating humility. When we try to deny our weaknesses, we delude ourselves into thinking that we're self-sufficient and have no real need for others, including God! But when we can accept that we can't stand alone, that we have needs, that we'll always be far from perfect, and that there is a hunger in our heart that we can't seem to satisfy on our own, we'll become "down to earth," and humility will flourish. Because of this, we can understand our weaknesses to be strengths, as they remind us of our need for God. That's why Saint Paul could say, "I will rather boast most gladly of my weaknesses, in order that the power of Christ may dwell with me" (2 Cor 12:9).

Part of being "down to earth" is being good soil, receptive to the seeds that God wishes to plant in us. The flip side of that coin is accepting that all we have, any good we might do, and any noble thing we achieve or accomplish is a gift from the hand of God. It's not we alone who do such things; it's God who does them in us and through us. And should we come to accept that, we'll find ourselves working and acting no longer for our glory, but for the glory of the Lord.

"What's your greatest weakness?" need not be a question to dread. Whatever the honest answer might be, we can rejoice that it's a key to growing in faith. That greatest weakness isn't a liability, as it can truly be our greatest strength, because through humility our humble God can bless us with both happiness and holiness. And so, as the English say, "Eat some humble pie." Or better yet, as Scripture says: "Humble yourselves before the Lord and he will exalt you" (Jas 4:10).

## CHAPTER 11

# Take a Flying Leap

When she was seven, I helped my eldest daughter learn to ride a two-wheeler. She was a bit frightened when we began. We'd run across a local playground together with one of my hands on her back seat and another on her handlebar. After we'd gained enough speed I'd let go, but after coasting a few feet, she'd hit the brakes and stop because she wanted the assurance of seeing me right at her side. My being there gave her confidence and stability. At the same time, she knew that at some point she'd need to ride by herself, as scary as that might seem. Eventually, she took a leap of faith and cycled off on her own.

In a manner of speaking, Jesus had to teach his disciples to ride on their own. For quite some time, they had lived alongside Jesus. They ate, drank, prayed, traveled, talked, and ministered with him. And all the while, Jesus had been teaching them about faith. But then it came time for them to put those faith lessons into practice, and Jesus sent them off in pairs, without him at their side. It had to happen sooner or later. After all, Jesus wasn't going to be with them forever.

The disciples' experience is our experience as well. Like them, we make our journey of faith without Jesus visibly at our side and are invited to believe in one whom we cannot see. And that can be challenging, even scary! We may find ourselves sympathizing with "Doubting Thomas," the apostle who insisted on seeing and even touching the resurrected Jesus before he would believe the excited claims of his friends that Jesus had risen from the dead. Like Thomas, we sometimes wish to see in order to believe, and we can find it comforting to know that even a handpicked companion of the Lord struggled with doubt and unbelief.

However, it isn't always possible for us to see what we're called to believe in. This doesn't mean, though, that belief is impossible. In fact, each one of us believes all sorts of things we cannot see; we accept quite a bit as real and true without having concrete proof. We do this because if we could accept only those things we could prove or personally experience, we could rely on very little. For instance, I'm happy to accept that there's a city in Africa named Timbuktu, even though I've never been there myself. Similarly, Saint Augustine once said that he had to "take it on faith" that the people who claimed to be his mother and father were indeed his parents!

Are we foolish to believe such things? Not if we think that those who tell us of them are believable. Nevertheless, we also know that we could prove them right or wrong if we wanted to. We could hop a plane and visit Timbuktu; a DNA test can determine parenthood. But what about Jesus? There's no test to prove his existence, let alone show that he is who he says he is. Without cold, hard proof, how can we believe in Jesus?

That's a question many of us struggle with. But while there may be no cold, hard proof, that's not to say that there isn't plenty of evidence. There are hints everywhere! For instance, there's the fact that things exist. *We* exist! Does that not suggest a Creator? Then there's creation itself: it's beautiful, complex, and ordered. Could all that be nothing more than a random fluke of nature? Not really. And what about us? We create, think, love, and have a hard-wired sense of right and wrong. Might that hint at a God in whose image we are made? But that's not all. Things happen to us that we just can't brush off as coincidence and wonder if they might be little miracles. And then there's the unbroken testimony of the Church down through the ages, beginning with those who knew Jesus himself.

Based on all this, it's certainly reasonable to believe! All that evidence adds up to a logical conclusion. We may not have the cold, hard proof we wish for, but if we wait for that, we may find ourselves sitting on the fence of unbelief for a long, long time. To get off the fence requires faith. Sometimes, it requires a flying leap of faith! And that can be hard! Thankfully, Jesus understands very well. That's why he said to "Doubting Thomas," and says to us: "Blessed are those who have not seen and have believed" (Jn 20:29).

But why does Jesus make us do this? Why doesn't he just appear to us and the whole world so that everyone would believe? If he really loves us, why doesn't he simply reveal himself and get it over with? Those are fair questions. But maybe love is the answer. Maybe Jesus loves us so much that he doesn't show himself to us because he wants us to love him back. Think of it this way: if Jesus unveiled his power and glory in such a way that left no room for doubt, we would be compelled to believe. We wouldn't have any choice! But Jesus wouldn't want that because the end of free choice eliminates the possibility of love. And true love is never forced. It's always a decision.

That's why Jesus speaks to us in whispers instead of shouts. Rather than crashing into us or hitting us over the head, he prefers to gently brush past us or tap us on the shoulder from behind. As opposed to forcing himself upon us, he extends to us an invitation and waits patiently for our response. Our answer will likely involve a leap of faith, which can be scary. True love, however, requires it. And if we take it, we'll one day realize that instead of falling, we have been caught in the arms of one who loves us before we ever thought of loving him.

# Part 2

# *Churchy Things to Do*

## CHAPTER 12

# Check into the Hospital

As I drive around town, I'll sometimes notice a rosary hanging from someone's rearview mirror, or maybe a "Jesus fish" decal on the back of another car. When I see things like that, I know that the driver is a Christian. I'm reminded that I am far from alone in being a disciple of Christ and that I am part of a worldwide family of brothers and sisters, united in bonds forged by the Holy Spirit, all loved by the same Father in heaven.

This family we know as the Church. It's a divine family! Yet it is made up of very frail men and women whose broken humanity sometimes obscures the holy. As can happen in any human family, relationships within the Church may become strained, or even shattered altogether. Some members drive one another crazy or find each other boring. Feelings get hurt, motives are misunderstood, dynamics become dysfunctional, and those who are supposed to love one another do exactly the opposite. There are sibling rivalries, breakups, "black sheep" who rebel, and the tragedies of neglect and abuse. Some pack their bags and fly the nest, looking for escape or adventure, rarely to come back, if ever. They may show up for the holidays, but mostly out of a sense of obligation or guilt.

Such experiences with our Church family lead some to wonder: Why bother? They can become mistrustful of institutional Christianity, and want little or even nothing at all to do with it. Perhaps they'll describe themselves as "spiritual" but not "religious." They want God but not Church; they wish to believe but not to belong. To be sure, the deeply-ingrained individualism of our culture is a contributing factor in this, and sometimes such thinking is merely an excuse for laziness or indifference. At the same time, good people can get put off for good reasons, and these days they often vote with their feet.

Perhaps we've thought of walking away as well. Maybe we've had it up to our eyeballs with disappointment in the Church for all sorts of understandable reasons. So why should we stay? What's the point? To put it bluntly: Jesus desperately wants us to, because he and the Church are one. The Church is the Body of Christ, and all we who have been baptized are members. In this Body, we're united to Jesus, and one another, by the Holy Spirit. In other words, the Church isn't just a group of people who have come together because they have a common devotion to Jesus. Instead, the Church is a divine institution into which Jesus himself has invited us. Should we separate ourselves from the Church, we'll find ourselves becoming, and feeling, more and more separated from Christ.

We need the Church because we need Christ. We also need the Church because we need each other. When Jesus first sent off his disciples to teach and heal, he didn't send them off alone, as isolated individuals. Instead, they went forth in pairs, two by two, so they could strengthen one another, serve one another, and challenge one another. As we make our journey of faith, Jesus doesn't want us to travel alone either. He wants us to have the companionship of our brothers and sisters. In other words, authentic Christianity isn't just a matter of "Jesus and me." It's also a matter of "Jesus and we."

It can be tempting to think otherwise. An often-shared story tells of an older, experienced Christian who was asked by a young person why one should remain in the Church. As it was, the two of them were in a living room, seated next to a roaring fire in a fireplace. To answer the question, the wise elder reached for a pair of tongs, removed a hot glowing coal from the fire, and held it up between them. For a brief moment, nothing seemed to happen. But within seconds, the coal stopped glowing, and it began to cool. Yet after it was returned to the fire, it began to glow once again. Without a word having been spoken, the young person understood the lesson.

People and experiences we encounter in the Church may indeed challenge our faith. Nevertheless, for our faith to be complete, we need to participate in the life of the Church. We need the support and encouragement of our fellow Christians; we need the prayers and witness of the communion of saints; we need to share our celebrations and rites of passage; we need sacramental grace and the authentic teaching of how Jesus revealed God to us; and we need the challenges that are part and parcel of communal Christian life—challenges that may call forth from us patience, pardon, courage, surrender, and the blessing of coming to see things from a horizon wider that our own.

To participate in the Church's life, however, may require that we lower our expectations; sometimes we'll need to forgive. As Scripture says, the Church includes both "wheat and weeds" (see Mt 13:26), or, in other words, saints and sinners. Because of this, the Church is always in need of reform. It always has been and always will be, this side of heaven. Should we view the Church through rose-colored glasses, we'll likely wind up disappointed.

Instead of writing off the Church as a "haven for hypocrites," however, it's far better to embrace it as a "hospital for sinners." Yes, at times we might wish to sue some of the hospital staff for malpractice, and our fellow patients can make us long for a private room! Nevertheless, the hospital itself is sound. Christ himself is the hospital administrator, and we can find solace and hope in the fact that he is in control. It's his Church, and he constantly guides it, cleanses it, and renews it. He promised, in fact, that "the gates of the netherworld shall not prevail against it!" (Mt 16:18). And if we can accept that, we would do well to stay checked in: for the health of our faith, for the health of our soul.

## CHAPTER 13

# Sweep Up the Crumbs

While a priest was deep in prayer at his desk, his secretary burst into his office. "Thank goodness," she exclaimed in relief, "I see you're not busy!" This joke suggests how easy it is to view prayer as unimportant, considering everything we have heaped on our plates.

So often our daily responsibilities and hectic routines seem to preclude time for prayer. Just getting through the day can be a major accomplishment! Everyone seems to be running around 24/7, and we wind up anxious, overburdened, and exhausted. When we feel this way, prayer becomes just one more box to check off on a "to do" list that's already way too long.

It doesn't help that our culture is burdened by a "bias toward busyness." Our world values who we know, how much we have, what we do, and what we look like doing it. In this climate, we fear losing our edge or falling behind. And since prayer doesn't seem to produce immediate results, let alone a product, we can dismiss it as a waste of effort or a luxury for those with too much time on their hands.

Jesus appreciates what we face; he knows what it's like to be busy. During his ministry, he was often in great demand. Crowds sought him out day and night. It seemed like everybody wanted something from him: a moment of his time, a word of wisdom, a healing touch. All the while, Jesus was on the move, traveling from town to town. Yet the Gospels tell us how, in spite of everything he had to do, Jesus would rise before dawn and pray in solitude. In doing so, he sets an important example for us.

Above all, Jesus prayed because he wanted to spend time with the Father he loved, just as the Father loved him in return. Catholic tradition understands this love as the Holy Spirit. Through the same Spirit, Jesus and the Father share this same love with us. Once we appreciate this, we'll understand that God invites us to prayer not to annoy us, inconvenience us, overburden us, or give us something to feel guilty about, but simply because he loves us so much.

God is constantly reaching out to touch our lives and bring us closer together. Faith is our response to this; it's the foundation of our relationship with God. And as with any relationship, communication is a key to success. For our relationship with God to be honest, fruitful, and deep, we need to communicate with God. We call this communication "prayer," and it's necessary for our faith's health. Understood this way, prayer isn't a waste of time. Instead, if we wish to have a strong faith, time spent in prayer is essential. After all, trust is established only with time. Love grows only with time. And mutual knowledge is built only over time.

Yet finding that time can be hard. Saint Francis de Sales once said that all of us should pray for a half hour each day, except when we're busy—and then we need an hour! But how on earth can we find a half hour a day for prayer—let alone an hour? Saint Francis himself gives us a hint: "Aspire often to God by short, burning elevations of the heart."[1] In other words, we can lift up little prayers to God during the little crumbs of time we have throughout our day. And should we gather all these crumbs together, we may be surprised to discover how much time for prayer we actually have!

Our days are filled with opportunities to meet God, think of him, speak with him, and listen to him. Never is there a situation or circumstance in which he is not present. Yet these golden moments can so easily slip through our hands, and God can slide right past us, totally unnoticed. So what can we do? Perhaps we might rise a few minutes earlier each morning or stay up a few minutes later each night, even just once or twice a week. Also, we can take advantage of those little quiet moments that punctuate our day: behind the steering wheel, over the stove, in the shower, waiting in the checkout line, and so forth. And if we're a runner or a walker, we might take a rosary along with us.

Another way to pray more is to make it a habit to pray at the beginning and the end of regular daily events. For instance, we can say a prayer when we first wake up, and again when we turn in for the night. We can also pray at the beginning and end of meals, during commutes to and from our jobs, and when starting and finishing our work. We can pray when we tuck our kids in, pray when we drop them off at school, and again when we pick them up.

Saint Paul encourages us to pray without ceasing! But that's not something that can happen overnight. It's best to start small and then build from there. As a popular slogan puts it, we should "pray as we can and not as we can't." Catholic author

Robert Wicks encourages people to pray at least two minutes a day. That advice is often received with skepticism because people generally feel that they owe more time to God than that. But Wicks explains that "simple constant deeds are always more meaningful than rarely fulfilled great promises."[2] And besides, everyone, without exception, can find at least two quality minutes a day to spend with the Lord.

Even a few daily moments of prayer, however, will set the stage for a deeper relationship with God. It will certainly strengthen our faith when it feels fragile! And we'll likely find that it will increase our desire to spend even more time with God. We'll also see, perhaps slowly at first, that our lives will have begun to change for the better. So sweep up all the little crumbs of time you have for prayer! They'll provide ample food to feed your faith.

## CHAPTER 14

# Get Soaked in Scripture

As a young man sixteen hundred years ago, Saint Augustine sought meaning and purpose in his life. He had been raised by a Christian mother, Saint Monica, and although he had drifted away from the Church, he was still fascinated by Jesus. That's why, in his quest for truth, he early on turned to the Bible. But as he read it, he felt disappointed. In its pages, he didn't find the scholarly philosophy he enjoyed reading. He found instead, especially in the Old Testament, tales of conflict and very imperfect people. It didn't help that he was reading a poor translation. Augustine concluded that the Bible was of no use to him, so he put his copy aside to gather dust.

Years later, in Milan, Italy, he encountered the magnificent preaching of Saint Ambrose, the local bishop. Ambrose's homilies led Augustine to view the Bible in an entirely new way, especially the Old Testament. Augustine came to appreciate that the Old Testament shouldn't be approached as a philosophy textbook, but as a reflection of the great sweep of God's plan in human history, culminating in Jesus himself. All of which the Old Testament spoke was but a journey toward Jesus.

The real turning point came when Augustine, sitting in a garden, heard what sounded like a child's voice urging him to "take up and read." A Bible was nearby. Augustine opened it and his eyes came to rest on words that cut him to the heart. At that moment, he knew that not only was Jesus the key to understanding the entire Bible, but that Jesus himself could speak with him through the Bible. In other words, the Bible wasn't simply a resource for understanding God; it was instead a book in which one could encounter God.

Elements of Saint Augustine's conversion story may strike a chord with us. Like him, many of us are looking for faith, or hoping to strengthen the faith we have. From time to time we may have turned to the Bible, seeking a clue or inspiration, but found it to be puzzling, overwhelming, unhelpful, or a turnoff. Perhaps, again like Augustine, the Bible we've picked up is a poor translation for our needs; that one in the hotel nightstand was translated four hundred years ago, after all! So we've written off the Bible as irrelevant, and our copy, should we have one, gathers dust.

Yet Saint Augustine ultimately met Jesus in the Bible, and we can too. How? Like him, we can "take up and read"—something we may not be used to doing. Earlier generations of Catholics weren't encouraged to read the Bible, and many Catholic homes didn't have one anyway. But times have changed, and from the highest levels Catholics are invited to learn what generations of Protestant Sunday School kids grew up singing: "Jesus loves me, this I know, for the Bible tells me so!"[1]

When we read the Bible, we may find ourselves confused. That's okay, and thankfully there are excellent resources available to help us view the Scriptures through a Catholic lens. The truth is, the Bible can't be completely understood outside the Church. Consider this: When he ascended into heaven, Jesus didn't leave behind a book; he left behind a Church, filled with the Holy Spirit. The Bible sprang from the Church as part of its living Tradition. For us to fully benefit from the Bible, it should be approached through the framework of the Church and its teaching.

Should we not have much time to read the Bible on our own, we can certainly hear it proclaimed on Sundays. Over any three-year period, great parts of the Bible are presented to us in the readings at Mass, called the "Liturgy of the Word." Just as those who listened to Jesus were astonished when he taught them during their worship, we can have the same experience when we worship, if we make the effort to pay careful attention to the Scriptures when they're proclaimed. We hear them through the voices of lectors or clergy. But it is God himself who speaks to us: "In the sacred books, the Father who is in heaven comes lovingly to meet his children and talks with them."[2]

On our journey of faith, we need food to sustain us and keep us going. Jesus understands this, and he gives us himself as nourishment. "I am the bread of life" (Jn 6:35), he said. These words refer not only to the gift of the Eucharist, but also to the unique teaching and divine wisdom he offers and through which we come to know God and his love for us. This "bread of life" comes to us today through the pages of the Bible, which we understand to be the word of God.

The Bible was inspired by God as no other written words have been or ever will be. Its books may have been written ages ago, but they speak of timeless truths and eternal wisdom, without which our faith can become vague or rootless. Scripture instructs, challenges, consoles, and helps diminish the distance between God and us. Without the Bible, we would know precious little about Jesus and what he revealed to us about God. "Ignorance of the Scriptures is ignorance of Christ," wrote Saint Jerome.[3] His words may sound blunt, but they're certainly true.

The good news is Jesus doesn't want us to be ignorant of him. To know him is to love him, and Jesus wants us to know and love him deeply. We might understand the Bible, then, as his gift of love to us, that we might come to love him in return, be strengthened in faith, and transformed into generous, compassionate people. In a word, to become more like him.

We might say, then, that in order to be immersed in a life of faith, it is good for us to be fully soaked in Scripture. Jesus says to us, as the child's voice said to Saint Augustine, "Take up and read."

## CHAPTER 15

# Take Bread for the Journey

While once teaching a group of young children, Sister Breige McKenna explained that Jesus would live in their hearts when they received their first Holy Communion. This came as a surprise to one girl, who asked if Jesus's furniture would be moving in with him![1] Well, there is no furniture involved, of course! But Jesus does come and live in our hearts through Holy Communion.

A woman at my former parish taught this truth to a boy with nonverbal autism who was preparing for his first Communion. She wanted to make sure that he could distinguish between the normal food he ate at meals and the spiritual food he would receive in Holy Communion. To do this, she sketched a big picture of his body on a sheet of brown paper. Where the stomach would be, she traced a circle and filled it with samples of food he would often eat, such as Cheerios and things like that. Next, she drew a picture of his heart and placed in it some unconsecrated communion wafers. After completing the picture, she asked the boy where the food he eats at meals goes. He pointed to his own stomach, and then the stomach on the big picture. Finally, she asked him where the spiritual food Jesus gives him goes, and he touched his heart, and then the one on the picture with the wafers. He was ready for his first Holy Communion!

"Even if all the physical hunger of the world were satisfied," Blessed Pope John Paul II wrote, "the deepest hunger of man would still exist."[2] He was referring to the hunger of our hearts—a hunger that can only be satisfied by Jesus.

Only Jesus can fulfill our need for meaning, commitment, depth, wholeness, and intimacy. This was learned by a woman I know who was fond of wearing a necklace with a heart-shaped pendant. The heart, however, wasn't solid. It was only the outline of a heart. She said that this pendant was symbolic of her own heart which she felt was empty. At times she had tried to fill her heart with various things—some good, some bad. But it was only when Jesus broke into her life that her heart really began to be nourished. "Our hearts are restless until they rest in thee,"[3] wrote Saint Augustine. But perhaps we can paraphrase him and say: Our hearts are hungry until they are fed by Jesus.

To feed our hungry hearts, Jesus gives us nothing less than the gift of himself. That's what, or more precisely, that's *who* we receive in Holy Communion. Jesus not only feeds our hearts, but he dwells in them with love. That's how Jesus himself explained it. When he taught about Communion, he spoke of giving his flesh for the life of the world. To share his life, he continued, we need to eat that flesh and drink his blood. And should we do that, he will "remain" in us and we in him, and we will live forever (see Jn 6: 51–57).

Through this teaching, Jesus tells us just how much he loves us. In effect, he's saying: "I give myself to you." "I want you to be with me, and I want to stay with you." "I want us to be together forever." "I love you so much that I'd die for you." This is the language of lovers! It's almost something you might expect to read in a romance novel. But it also happens to be the language of our faith. As the *Catechism of the Catholic Church* reminds us: "Our Savior instituted the Eucharistic sacrifice of his Body and Blood . . . to entrust to his beloved Spouse, the Church . . . a sacrament of love."[4] And that's a direct quote!

This means that whenever we present ourselves for Holy Communion, Jesus says to us: "I love you!" More than that, he actually fills us with his love; he nourishes us with a love that comes to us under outward signs of bread and wine. It's for good reason, then, that one of the traditional titles for the Mass is the "Holy Eucharist." Eucharist comes from two Greek words: *eu* meaning "good" and *charis* meaning "gift." The Eucharist, then, is Jesus' "good gift." And what greater gift could Jesus give us than the gift of himself?

In addition to being a "good gift," Holy Communion is also a necessary gift if we wish for our faith to grow. We ask for it whenever we pray the Our Father and say: "Give us this day our daily bread." With these words, we aren't just asking that God provide us with essential things like food, clothing, and shelter. The word we translate as "daily" is a rare Greek word found nowhere else in the Bible. It means "super-essential" or "more than essential." And it refers to the bread-become-Jesus in the Eucharist.

It's good to think of the Eucharist as "daily bread" because we need its nourishment for our daily lives. The struggles and temptations we face each day can easily weaken our faith, which is why we need the strength, healing, forgiveness, and peace Jesus offers us in Holy Communion. That's also why, when our faith feels fragile, it's a good idea to receive Holy Communion as often as we can.

Our faith life is something like a race, Saint Paul tells us—an endurance run in which we need to persevere and keep our eyes on our heavenly goal (see 1 Cor 9:24). And as any runner will tell you, one must eat well to run well! There's the carbo-loading before the starting gun, the energy gels while running, and the traditional bagel and banana afterward for muscle recovery. The same is true for our faith "run." To run it well, we need the food which is the Eucharist.

A popular invitation to Mass reads, "Jesus of Nazareth requests the honor of your presence at a banquet to be given in his honor next Sunday morning." Let's accept that invitation to receive bread for our journey and food for our faith.

 CHAPTER 16

# Read a Book

An old tale speaks of Saint Augustine walking along the seashore, deep in thought, trying to wrap his mind around the doctrine of the Trinity. He came across a child, who was filling a hole in the sand with buckets of water. When Saint Augustine asked what the child was doing, "I'm trying to pour the ocean into this hole," was the reply. "That's impossible!" said Saint Augustine with a smile. "No more impossible than your trying to comprehend the Trinity," observed the child, who promptly vanished.

We can't fully comprehend the mystery of the Trinity either. It's just not possible! We can understand to a certain extent, but the full magnitude of who God is will always remain beyond us this side of heaven. I'll never forget how a seminary professor of mine approached a chalkboard and announced, "This chalkboard is God." But he then drew a small chalk dot and said, "This is what we understand about God."

Even Jesus' family and friends sometimes didn't understand who he was, or what he was about. When the angel Gabriel announced to Mary that she would conceive Jesus by the Holy Spirit, she wondered aloud, "How can this be?" And upon hearing Jesus speak of eating his flesh and drinking his blood, some of his followers threw up their hands and walked off, complaining that his words were too hard to understand. The disciples were puzzled too, but they didn't walk away. "Where would we go?" Peter asked Jesus. "You have the words of everlasting life!" (see Jn 6:68). He continued to follow Jesus, even though there was much he didn't understand.

Peter's example can inspire us. We too may not understand everything our faith calls us to believe. But the last thing our Lord wants us to do is to stomp off in frustration. Jesus invites us to keep following him that we might come to better know who he is and the God he reveals. Jesus very much wants to be rightly understood. That much was clear when he once asked his disciples about who people thought he was. He received a variety of answers, but on this occasion Peter wasn't puzzled at all: "You are the Christ," he exclaimed, "the Son of the Living God!" (see Mt 16:16 *RSV*).

Yet even then, Peter didn't have the complete picture. Because just moments later, when Jesus announced that he would be tortured and executed, Peter was utterly appalled. He correctly identified Jesus as the Christ, but what he didn't understand, at that time, was that being the Christ would lead to his suffering and death.

Like Peter, many of us operate with a limited appreciation of who Jesus is. I have a suspicion that when we meet him face to face at the end of our lives, we'll be astounded by the full reality of our Lord. In the meantime, our images of Jesus in particular, and God in general, need to be constantly revisited, challenged, and revised.

To do this, it's helpful to consider where our images of God may have come from. For instance, culture can shape our image. Victorian England was scandalized by Millais's painting, "The Carpenter's Shop," that depicted Jesus and his family as rustic and poor—just as Scripture and historians tell us they were.[1] Yet certain class-conscious English of that era refused to accept God's Son portrayed in such a way. Likewise, our materialistic, fast-paced, self-centered, and superficial culture can disfigure our image of the Lord.

In addition, our parents play a significant role in shaping our image of God. Their attitudes, prejudices, ways of handling stress, work habits, intelligence, and temperament all contribute. Distant parents suggest a distant God; angry parents evoke an angry God; happy parents reflect a joyful God, and so forth. Conscious of this, we might honestly reflect on how our parents may have influenced how we understand God.

Sometimes our image of God is simply a projection of ourselves. This might result in a "god" who never challenges us and smiles upon everything we do. It might also result in a "god" who too much reflects our anger and incapacity to forgive. This "god" is quick to punish and slow to pardon, is easy to fear but hard to love.

God invites us to grow in our understanding of who he is. And that's where our faith comes in, because there's much we couldn't begin to understand of God if we didn't first have faith, since faith enables us to see things as God sees them. In other words, to understand God, we need to believe in God. Or as Saint Augustine once confessed: "I believe in order to understand."[2] Faith and understanding go hand in hand. Faith is required for understanding, but understanding can strengthen our faith.

That's why studying what our Catholic faith calls us to believe can bolster our faith when it feels fragile. We are transformed through the renewal of our minds (see Rom 12:2)! Since we're made in God's image to love and serve him, ignorance of who God is or what he wants for us can lead us to live misguided lives. As Christians, we're to imitate Christ. But if we don't really know who Christ is, how can we imitate him? Lack of knowledge can blind us and shackle us. Yet Jesus himself assures us that the truth will set us free (see Jn 8:32).

To enjoy the freedom that truth brings, we can study and learn the truth. Indeed, is there any other subject that's more important? After all, the soul of education should be the education of the soul. So read good Catholic books! Join a Catholic book club or a Bible study. Participate in religious education programs. Watch videos. Listen to podcasts. Take a class. Endless opportunities are available!

We'll never be able to absorb all there is to know. We can't get the heavens inside our head, wrote G. K. Chesterton, so we can be content to get our heads inside the heavens.[3] And that's okay because God is not a subject to be mastered, a puzzle to be solved, or a scientific specimen to be examined. He is a Mystery to be adored, a Creator to be worshiped, a Savior to be praised, and the source and object of our faith—a faith that will grow, along with what we know.

 CHAPTER 17

# Don't Read a Book

As he sat down to eat in his university's dining hall, Saint John Cantius (1390–1473) saw a beggar outside. Without hesitation, Saint John rushed out and gave the man his dinner. When he returned to his seat, Saint John's plate was once again filled with food, but not, apparently, by human hands. Later, a tradition arose to recall this miracle. Each day, a poor man was brought to the dining hall for dinner, and his arrival was announced with the words, "A poor man is coming!" But immediately afterward, another voice would cry out with a correction: "Jesus Christ is coming!"

Why was this done? Because Jesus taught that he himself is encountered in the poor. Indeed, he insisted that whenever we serve the poor, we serve him as well. It would make sense then, that if we're looking to strengthen our faith in Jesus, we should search for him where he promises he can be found. This was the advice given to a young German student who approached a

*69*

prominent Catholic scholar, Karl Rahner, for advice on what books might restore his failing faith. "No books!" Rahner replied. Instead, he recommended, "Go and serve the poor in Munich and your faith will be rekindled."[1]

Books can be a very important ingredient for our growth in faith. But our faith needs more than just study to be strong. It also needs to be put into action, especially in service to the needy and poor. In fact, it can be argued that such action is far more important than study. As Thomas à Kempis (1380–1471) wrote in his famous *Imitation of Christ*, "At the Day of Judgment we shall not be asked what we have read, but what we have done."[2]

Sometimes, however, we can resist what Jesus invites us to do. I recall how once, during my morning commute, I saw in a church doorway a rough-looking homeless man who had obviously spent the night there. As I passed by in my comfortable car, sipping my hot cup of coffee, I'll confess that my first thought was: "Thank God, I don't have to deal with *that*!"

Yet Jesus calls us to deal with *that*—or deal with *them*, to be more precise—if we truly wish to deal with *him*. Through so much of his ministry, Jesus makes it quite clear that service to the needy and poor is a nonnegotiable element for a strong faith.

On one occasion, a large crowd was following Jesus while a man named Bartimaeus begged by the side of the road (see Mk 10:46–52). When he heard that Jesus was passing by, the beggar cried out for help. But the crowd told Bartimaeus to be quiet. They didn't want to hear him! And they didn't want Jesus to hear him either.

Jesus ultimately did hear Bartimaeus because the beggar kept yelling! But do we hear the cries of the poor? Perhaps we don't want to hear, like the crowds didn't wish to hear

Bartimaeus. For them he was a distraction, a nuisance, an inconvenience. Maybe he made them feel uncomfortable, ashamed, or guilty. Perhaps he stank or looked shabby, and they were "grossed out." Sometimes we're tempted to feel the same way. A homeless person approaches our car at the stoplight, and we stare straight ahead while gripping the steering wheel. Appeals come in the mail with pictures of wide-eyed children with bloated bellies, and we automatically toss the appeals with the catalogs. We turn a blind eye, or figure that it's somebody else's problem.

Even Jesus' disciples fell for this temptation. Once, after thousands of people had spent the day in the wilderness listening to Jesus, the disciples wanted to send them home for dinner. But Jesus, knowing that there would be little dinner for them at home, had a different idea. "You give them something to eat" (Lk 9:13, *RSV*), he said.

The disciples were stunned. They protested that no food was to be had, except for a handful of loaves and fishes offered by a young boy. But that was enough for Jesus. He accepted the boy's gift, blessed it, broke it, shared it with the crowd, and everyone ate until they were full. They even had leftovers.

Whenever we encounter the poor, Jesus speaks to us the same words he spoke to his disciples: "You give them something to eat." Like the disciples, we might protest that there's not much we're able to do, but, as the little boy's bread and fish remind us, nothing is too little in God's service, as he can do great things with the smallest of gifts. And we almost always have something to share. God doesn't ask us to do the impossible! He just asks that we do what we can.

And we can do many things. To begin with, we can pray. We can pray for global justice and a fair distribution of the world's resources. We can pray for the needy people we encounter throughout our day—people with faces and names. And we can prayerfully examine our lifestyles, our financial priorities, and our stewardship of God's blessings that we might live more simply that others may simply live.

We can give of our time, talent, and treasure to food pantries, refugee assistance centers, crisis pregnancy programs, soup kitchens, and homeless shelters. We can mentor, tutor, repair houses, or become a foster or adoptive parent. To the best of our ability, we can lend our financial support to relief agencies. We can always treat with courtesy and respect those who ask our help. Finally, we can weigh our society's responsibility to care for its poorest members every time we cast a vote.

We need to be careful not to serve the poor simply to grow in faith. The poor are people created in God's image and through whom we encounter Jesus—not a means to an end! Yes, increased faith can come from service, but that's the by-product, not the goal. Nevertheless, we won't enjoy that by-product until we serve. So what are we to do? Open a book? Better yet, let's open our hearts and roll up our sleeves.

## CHAPTER 18

# Look Over Your Shoulder

Do you have tokens which remind you of the love that others have for you? Things like photos of family or friends in your workplace? A box of old letters? Maybe a picture one of your children made for you, or a homemade gift? Or what about a souvenir from a special day with a special someone? I'll let you in on a professional secret: I know more than one priest who keeps "thank you" notes that have been sent to him over the years and who pulls them out to read after a tough day when he could use a reminder that he's loved.

Everyone treasures being told that they're loved. Radio personality Garrison Keillor tells a joke about a stereotypically reserved Norwegian farmer who loved his wife so much that he almost told her once! But the truth is that saying "I love you" can be deeply important to a relationship's health. That's why marriage experts encourage spouses to tell each other every day, "I love you." That's why parenting experts advise moms and dads to tell their kids every day, "I love you." And that's why God communicates his love for us every day too.

God seeks to remind us that he loves us because we can forget that he does. Sometimes we forget because of the *busyness of life*. We've got too many things going on. We get distracted. Jesus fades into the background—out of sight and out of mind. At other times it's the *pleasures of life* that lead us to forget. Our pleasures make us content and comfortable. Life is smooth sailing; the world is our oyster. We lose sight of our need for God, and we forget about his love. The *pains of life* can also make us forget, especially when our pain is all we can think about. We may not forget about God at times like this, but we can certainly doubt his love. We forget that it's always there.

Our faith suffers when we lose sight of God's love for us. That's one reason why Jesus gave us the Holy Eucharist. The Eucharist is many things and has layers of meaning. But at a very basic, fundamental level, the Eucharist is a reminder—perhaps the supreme reminder—of God's love. Think back to the Last Supper, the first Eucharist. Jesus took bread, broke it, gave it to his disciples, and said, "Do this in *memory* of me" (Lk 22:19). He said the very same words again over the cup of wine. Evidently, he wants us to remember.

Sometimes, when I'm celebrating the Eucharist, and I'm holding the Body of Christ in my hands, or gazing into the chalice filled with the Precious Blood, and I speak those words of Jesus—"This is my body, given up for you; this is my blood, shed for you" (see Mt 26:28)—I can be overwhelmed by the magnitude of what Jesus did for me, and I'm reminded of how much he loves me. I'm also reminded of how much I need to be reminded!

Our Lord invites us to remember those times he's shown his love for us, especially when our faith is challenged or feels weak. He wishes for us to hang on to these memories when the going gets rough so we can find strength through them. A famous song from *The Sound of Music* encourages us to remember a few of our "favorite things" whenever we're hurting or afraid so we won't "feel so bad." All things considered, this is pretty good advice. It's far better, however, for us to remember a few of the times we've been touched by God's love.

My wife and I have found this to be true whenever we face a rough patch in our marriage or family life. We can recall how the Lord has intervened in our relationship in the past, bringing us together to become a sacrament, healing our wounds, teaching us lessons, challenging our fears, correcting our faults, making us stronger. When we remember these things, we know that we'll make it though our present crisis because of what the Lord has done for us before.

Has there been a time in your life, or even a particular moment, when God seemed very real and present to you? When you were sure you heard the voice of God speak? When God reached down and tapped you on the shoulder (or whacked you on the head)? When the truths of our religion became crystal clear and made perfect sense? When God was nearby, like a friend, guiding you, protecting you, challenging you? Perhaps a prayer was answered, you were brushed by grace, God whispered to you through a song or a book, or God used a situation or another person to nudge your life in a certain direction. If so, the Lord invites you to hold these memories dear and keep them in mind.

Even if you haven't had or can't recall such an experience, you can always remember that God embraced you as his child when you were baptized, that you've been filled with God's own life through the sacraments, and that Jesus died and rose again so you might have hope to live with him forever. "It is important not to lose this memory of God's presence in our lives," Pope Benedict XVI stressed. Such memories, he adds, are a "star of hope that gives us confidence."[1] Looking back to a "star of hope" doesn't mean being stuck in the past or trying to re-create old experiences or feelings. Instead, we look over our shoulder to be blessed with a stronger faith for the road ahead.

"It's hard to pray in the name of a Love one's forgotten," T. S. Eliot is said to have lamented, which is why God never wants us to forget his love. He invites us to recall the times he's broken into our lives, whenever we feel our faith is broken. Because whenever we find ourselves in darkness, we can always cherish our glimpses of the Light.

 CHAPTER 19

# Take the Long View

If someone were to ask you what you imagine heaven to be like, what would you say? Would you describe heaven as something of a celestial day spa, with soothing music and relaxing messages? Or in your mind is heaven like an island resort, with sandy beaches and fruity drinks? Maybe for you heaven is a "field of dreams" where your major league fantasies will finally come true. Or is heaven simply a place where all your bills are paid and you can catch up on sleep?

Perhaps you have questions about what heaven will be like. Will dogs be there (I happen to think so!)? And what will we do? As one bumper sticker proclaims: "If there's no golf in heaven, I'm not going!" Some of us fear that heaven will be boring—an eternity of monotony surrounded by chubby cherubs with harps on clouds. Maybe this is why one woman I saw wore a t-shirt that read: "Good girls go to heaven. Bad girls go to Vegas!"

Thankfully, the reality of heaven is very different from what we sometimes imagine it to be. To be sure, we'll never totally understand what heaven is like until we get there ourselves, God willing. However, there are some very important things we do understand about heaven—and they can help us to imagine heaven as a place where we'd want to be.

First and foremost, we will be with God in heaven, and with God we will find perfect happiness—the pure, lasting happiness that always seems to elude us in this life. There is no need for faith in heaven because we will see God face to face. We call this the "beatific vision," and it will fill us with joy. "How great will your glory and happiness be," exclaimed Saint Cyprian, "to be allowed to see God!"[1]

Also, since in heaven we will see God, we will also know love because God is love. Our world is filled with loneliness, war, hatred, resentment, and backstabbing competition. Our relationships, as good as they might be, are always compromised by sin, selfishness, pride, and immaturity. We inevitably hurt the ones we love. But not in heaven! There, we will love and be loved perfectly, with no strings attached or fingers crossed behind the back. In heaven, no one is rejected, used, abandoned, or hurt, because heaven is full of God's peace, harmony, forgiveness, healing, and joy. In heaven, love will truly mean never having to say we're sorry. And to top it off, we'll finally be able to love those we once loved to hate.

Heaven will be many things—things we can only begin to comprehend now. But we can safely say that whatever it will be like, it will exceed our wildest expectations, and it certainly won't be boring. The reality of heaven may be far removed from how we've pictured it in our imaginations, but it will satisfy and fulfill the deepest longings of our human hearts

—longings often expressed through what we might call "seeds of eternity" that are planted within each of us.

These seeds sprout in a variety of ways. We see something beautiful, and we're inspired. We meet someone truly noble and good and think, "I want to be like that." We ache to be loved for who we are. We want to be understood, appreciated, and valued. We expect life to have purpose and meaning. We want our world to be filled with fairness, happiness, and peace. Yet when we reflect on life's realities, we get the sense that things aren't the way they should be. People die young, and we think they're cheated of something. We encounter hatred, suffering, and injustice, and we protest: "That's not right! That's not fair!" And when we do, we're absolutely correct because we were made for something far better than this. We were made for heaven.

Keeping that truth in view will lead us to take the long view on life. Because when we keep in mind that this life isn't all there is, and that something better awaits us, our perspective on life will change. We'll be encouraged that our existence isn't a futile race against time; we'll be assured that death doesn't have the final word; we'll not get sucked into the dead-end mentality of "eat, drink, and be merry, for tomorrow we die." The difficulties and disappointments we encounter today won't completely crush us because we'll see them as but speed bumps and detours along the way to a final destination. In short, keeping heaven in view will fill us with hope. And because hope and faith are kissing cousins, our faith will grow stronger as eternity draws closer.

Longing for heaven isn't an escape from this world. Nor will focusing on the next life lead us to avoid dealing with the problems we face in this one. Living in hope of heaven actually leads us to live better lives, not just for our benefit, but for the benefit of those around us. Belief in heaven is a powerful motivation for us to do the right thing. Think of it this way: If this life is all there is, what's the point in being good? Why forgive those who hurt us? Why love our enemies? Why be chaste? Why give our money to charity? Why try to be a saint when it's easier, and seemingly more fun, to be a sinner? Why not be selfish? Why? Because as Catholics our hope for the next life depends on how we live this one, and we can appreciate that how we live in hope of heaven will sometimes lead us to create a little bit of heaven here on earth.

In this life, we may at times look around us and think: "Is this all there is?" But in heaven we'll look around us and exclaim: "It doesn't get any better that this!" With that hope in view, we can say with Saint Bernadette of Lourdes: "I shall do everything for heaven, my true home."[2]

 CHAPTER 20

# Flatter Sincerely

Imagine my wife's surprise when, after a Mass on All Saints Day, a bishop walked straight up to her and said with a smile: "Be a saint." As she did not know this bishop, she was surprised, to say the least! But she took the message to heart as a serious call to holiness, as well she should have since Jesus invites all of us to be saints. That's the reason why God created us in the first place.

But just what is a saint? A young boy once asked this question of a priest as they stood together in church. The priest pointed to the saints in the stained glass windows and said, "The saints are those people who let God's light shine through." God's light can shine through us too, and there's nothing complicated about it. As Saint Francis de Sales recommends, all we need to do is imagine ourselves to be in Jesus' presence, ask what we must do to be like him, and then do it.

Sometimes, however, we conclude that it's easier to admire saints from a distance than it is to be a saint ourself. We view sainthood like my neighbors viewed an old-fashioned push lawnmower I used to own. "Good for you!" one neighbor said to me. "That's so friendly to the environment!" Upon hearing the gentle whirr of the blades as I mowed, a dog walker said nostalgically, "Ah, the sounds of summer." A jogger passing by commented, "Boy! You really get a good workout using that!" And friends across the street said it was nice that they could enjoy drinks on their patio while I mowed, instead of being drowned out by a noisy gas engine. I noticed, however, that none of my neighbors purchased a push-mower of their own. I was often admired but never imitated.

The same could be said about the saints. They too are often admired but seldom imitated. Consider Jean Vanier. He's widely respected around the world for having founded L'Arche, an international organization for persons with intellectual disabilities, and he was personally honored by Blessed John Paul II. When interviewed on TV, he was told that many people referred to him as a saint. He didn't care for that, however. He said that sometimes people label other people saints because they don't want to try to be saints themselves. They think it's too hard or only for a special, heroic few.

Whenever we think that we could never be a saint, it's good to be reminded that saints aren't born, they're made! And some of those people God made into saints had a long way to go when they started. Their witness can remind us that there's hope for us too: if they can become saints, then we can as well. As Pope Benedict has written, "[The saints'] human and spiritual experience shows that holiness is not . . . an impossible goal for an ordinary person."[1] There's no such thing as a "hopeless sinner" because every sinner can hope to become a saint. Or to put it another way: Every saint has a past and every sinner has a future.

But when our faith feels fragile, we may wonder: Why bother pursuing sainthood when we're not entirely convinced it's worth the effort? Why consider the possibility? Because it sure beats the alternative! Try to imagine the person you would be without a shred of faith and without guidance from the Christian principles of love, kindness, generosity, and forgiveness. I have, and the picture that comes to mind isn't pretty. I completely understand Saint Vincent de Paul when he confessed that if it weren't for God's grace, he would have been "hard and repellent, rough and crabbed."[2]

At the same time, have you ever imagined yourself as a saint—a person filled with peace, hope, and love, rich in faith and good works? I've done this too. And even though I recognize that I have a long way to go to achieve this goal, I know it's possible if I live my life in union with Jesus. To live in imitation of Christ is the pathway to sharing the joy of Christ. And deep down, this is what we all want at the end of the day.

Jesus once contrasted a life lived with him and a life lived without him (Jn 15:1–11). He stressed that when we "remain" in him, we bear good fruit in our lives and glorify God. But when we don't remain in him, it's as if we wither and die. Without faith in Jesus, life's fullness and purpose elude us, and our lives can become directionless and disordered.

We do well to keep these two possibilities always before us as we choose how to live our lives. We can imagine the Christless image of ourselves and think, "There, but for the grace of God, go I." And we can picture ourselves as a saint and hope, "That, with the grace of God, is what I can become."

When picturing ourselves as a saint, we can look for guidance from the lives of the saints who have gone before us. By considering their stories, we'll be guided and instructed in how to become saints ourselves. How they lived out their faith in often challenging situations can inspire us to live out our faith in the challenging situations we face.

If we aren't familiar with the lives of the saints, being introduced to them can be a rich blessing. If we bear a saint's name, we can begin with him or her. At the same time, there are countless men and women, although not officially recognized as saints, who have lived lives rich in faith and holiness. Perhaps we know one or know of one. Their witness, and even friendship, can inspire us too.

It's often been said that imitation is the sincerest form of flattery. The saints don't seek to be flattered, but they won't mind being imitated because their lives will point us to Jesus. And that can only help to increase our fragile faith.

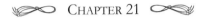 CHAPTER 21

# Shed Some Baggage

Children making their first confessions sometimes struggle with the traditional "Act of Contrition," the prayer offered to show that one is truly sorry. More than once I've heard "I am *hardly* sorry" instead of the correct words "I am *heartily* sorry." On one occasion, however, a young girl whose first confession I'd just heard offered the Act of Contrition flawlessly. "Good job!" I told her, and then raised my hand over her to begin the prayer of absolution. But she misunderstood what I was doing, and stood up and slapped my hand! All I could do was smile. She smiled too.

"High fives" aren't a standard part of the confession ritual, nor do I think they ever will be. Nevertheless, such a joyful and affirming act is certainly appropriate when one's sins are forgiven. Jesus himself said that the angels in heaven rejoice whenever we repent and turn our lives around (see Lk 15:10). Since that's the case, making a confession can be an occasion of joy, and something we look forward to. But for many people, confession is something to dread—if they bother to go at all.

As I was leaving a confessional on a Saturday afternoon, a person turned to me and said, "Father, I just have to ask … how much business do you get in here?" This question reflects the fact that far fewer Catholics make their confessions today than a generation ago. But why is this? Maybe they've had a bad experience in the past with a cold or angry or foolish priest. There are those who don't see the need for confession because they haven't heard it stressed or preached about. For some, the "old way" seemed too mechanical or impersonal, and they haven't bothered to come back. Also, it's been my experience that many people today are looking for an adult experience of reconciliation and not the same thing they had in second grade. When they don't find that, they don't bother. Changing notions of God and sin can play a factor too.

Some of us are too embarrassed, ashamed, or afraid. The prospect of confession would require confronting something in our past about which we're deeply troubled, and it seems easier and less painful to just ignore it. Perhaps we fear that God would treat us with condemnation, rejection, and scorn. Maybe we're convinced that we've done something too awful for even God to forgive, or that our habits or way of living have led us to be beyond help—and thus beyond God's mercy.

Others, however, just don't see a need for confession. We may think, "Overall, I'm a good person. I don't do anything that wrong. So why should I bother?" In other words, since we're decent, well-intentioned, fundamentally responsible human beings, there's no real reason to go to confession. With this understanding, confession isn't for those who are "basically good." It's only for those who are "basically bad."

The risk, however, is that should we focus exclusively on our good qualities, we lose sight of the fact that, this side of heaven, everybody sins—including us. And that's a danger. "When we forget we are sinners," warned Blessed Pope John Paul II, "we forget our need for Christ. And when we forget we need Christ, we have lost everything."

To which we could add: If we forget our need for Christ, our faith will evaporate. Acknowledging and confessing our sins, then, is essential for a healthy and growing faith.

It can also be a rich blessing for us! For starters, there's a huge psychological benefit to confession. One study has shown that Catholics who go to confession feel less guilt than other people. This may be because in confession we reveal our deepest, darkest secrets and then hear the words that God forgives and heals us. These words are very powerful indeed! Confession can also help us break those bad habits and attitudes that we just can't seem to shake. We try to get rid of them, but can't, and find ourselves in a repeating cycle of "good intention-failure-guilt." But when we confess these bad habits, we bring them to the surface, and healing can begin. It's a bit like the beginning of any Twelve Step program, in which one admits out loud that he or she has a problem. We all have our struggles, and a first step in moving beyond them is to admit them out loud in the sacrament of Confession. According to poet John Berryman, we're only as sick as our secrets. So what's the solution? Confession, not repression!

My wife compares her experience of confession with a mess we used to have in our family room. There was a cabinet there that held a TV, two speakers, a telephone, a computer and its monitor, a cassette player, a stereo receiver, a CD player, a VCR, and a turntable. The back of the cabinet was a chaotic, spaghetti-like tangle of cords, plugs, and wires. Stephanie said that before her confession, she felt as if her soul was like that crazy, tangled mess—all mixed up and out of sorts. After confession, however, she felt as if everything had been straightened out, neatened up, and put in its proper place. I know exactly what she's talking about.

Feelings like that are worthy of high fives! And God is happy for us to have them. We need not fear approaching him in confession because he will always be waiting for us with patience, compassion, and open arms. And there's nothing he won't or can't forgive! When he looks upon us, he's fully aware of our sins and brokenness. He sees someone who needed redeeming and who is in need of guidance and grace. But more than that, he sees someone he loves. And should we confess our sins, we give him an opportunity to demonstrate just how much he loves us by showering us with his mercy. Should we not confess, we're not cheating God in some way. We're only cheating ourselves! Of love. Of forgiveness. Of faith.

 CHAPTER 22

# Thanks for Sharing

An acquaintance of mine works in a very tense office environment. Yet in spite of the stress she faces, she's always been able to maintain her composure and a sense of peace on the job. During one especially hard day, a colleague came to her in tears and asked how she was able to handle all the negativity in their workplace. My acquaintance explained that she could do so only on account of her Catholic faith. As it was, she was on her way to the lunchtime Mass at the nearby cathedral, and she invited her coworker to come along. One year later, that coworker was baptized at Easter, and my acquaintance was her sponsor.

"Faith," Saint Paul explains, "comes from what is heard" (Rm 10:17). This means that for us to have a measure of faith, we must have heard something, somewhere, and from someone about God and his love for us. Perhaps what we heard came through family, friends, a teacher, clergy, an author, the pages of Scripture, the teachings of a saint, a media figure, or, as with the case of my acquaintance, a coworker. Quite possibly it came from a combination of these—if not all of the above! I love that Scripture speaks of how Saint Timothy came to faith through the witness of Lois and Eunice—his mother and grandmother (see 2 Tm 1:5).

At the same time, it may be that the Lord is inviting us to share our faith with another, just as faith has been shared with us. In fact, it's likely that he is, whether we're aware of it or not. There may very well be people in our lives whom the Lord might be able to reach only through us. Sharing our faith is called "evangelization." That's not a word Catholics have been accustomed to using, but evangelization is at the very heart of Catholicism: "She [the Church] exists in order to evangelize!" insisted Pope Paul VI.[1] And doing it isn't as hard or as scary as it may sound. "Evangelization" comes from the Greek words for "good news." To evangelize, then, is simply to share the good news at the heart of our faith.

But what if our faith feels fragile? Isn't it hypocritical to share our faith when its foundation feels shaky? Wouldn't doing so lead to more harm than good? Not at all! As Blessed Pope John Paul II assures us, *"Faith is strengthened when it is given to others!"*[2] This is true even when we fear that we don't have much faith to give because God can do amazing things with even the smallest of gifts, like feeding an entire crowd with a handful of loaves and fishes.

A shared faith is a strengthened faith for a number of reasons. To start, sharing our faith forces us to examine what it is we really believe, instead of taking it for granted—and that's always a good thing! It can lead us to recall positive faith experiences that we may have forgotten over time, and we can be inspired and renewed by the knowledge that God might be using us as his agent to enter into another's life. And if our faith feels fragile, that may be exactly what another person needs to hear. Our honesty may assure them that they're not alone with their questions, and our common struggle might bring us closer to each other and to God.

Sharing faith involves sharing our story. And we all have one! You wouldn't likely be reading this book if you didn't think God had touched your life in some way. Your story may not be dramatic, but that doesn't make it less real. In your faith journey, you may have had ups and downs, struggles and joys, periods of doubt, and moments of great certainty. You may have walked hand in hand with God, and run away from him as fast as you could. Sometimes God has seemed like a stranger, while at other times he was very present, very real. He has taught us hard lessons and wiped away our tears. He has both confused us and guided us. He has brought us to our knees and made us jump for joy. He has spoken to us through other people, through the pages of books, and in those special moments we know weren't coincidences but instead were brushes with grace. Maybe we've thought that God was unfair, maybe we've tried to tell him how to do his job, and maybe we've had no choice other than to trust him. At times we could have cared less about God, and at times we couldn't have cared more. Sometimes we've just gone through the motions, and sometimes we've been driven by love. And then there are those memories we hold dear—of first Holy Communion, of our grandmother who prayed the rosary, of the special teacher or nun who made a difference, of that retreat that changed the course of our life. All of these things we can share with others that they might be challenged and consoled, instructed and inspired.

Our Lord doesn't wish for us to keep our faith to ourselves. Faith is his gift to us, to be sure, but it's a gift he wants us to share. It's good if Jesus is in our hearts, because that's where he wants to be! But Jesus also wants to be in our workplaces, our schools, our neighborhoods, our homes. And we are the only people who can bring him there.

That's why Jesus spoke of us as being the "light of the world" (Jn 8:12). He insisted that we aren't to hide our light but allow it to shine for everyone to see, because he wants the light our faith can bring to dispel the darkness from the lives of those around us. And that can begin to happen, even if our faith's light is only a tiny spark. God can coax that spark into a roaring blaze—for others' lives and for ours.

 CHAPTER 23

# Don't Have a Cow

As odd as it may sound, fasting has become fashionable and is undergoing something of a revival! Today, some fast in the form of a hunger strike to make a political statement. Others fast because they insist that a low-calorie diet will help them live longer. There is even a posh clinic in Germany where it's joked that people pay thousands of dollars a week not to eat. Under medical supervision, guests fast to improve their overall health and remove toxins from their body.

An Internet search will reveal all sorts of Web sites and blogs about fasting. Many refer to "globesity"—the World Health Organization's label for the global health crisis of people who are overweight or obese. As Catholics, it is good for us to be concerned about this issue. Gluttony, which is overindulgence in food and drink, is one of the traditional "capital" sins. Our bodies are God's gift; Scripture calls them "temples of the Holy Spirit." We're called to take care of them by making healthy choices. When we do, we not only benefit ourselves, we also benefit those we love and who may depend on us.

But while it may have recently become popular with some, Catholics have been fasting since the foundation of the Church. Jesus fasted, and he spoke about fasting often. Today, we're called to fast on Ash Wednesday and Good Friday, and to abstain from meat on the Fridays of Lent. Some choose to abstain from other foods or extend their fasting beyond the minimum required. And this can certainly help anyone lose weight! But losing weight is not why Catholics fast.

We also don't fast because it's a Catholic cultural "badge," or to prove our holiness to God or anyone else. We fast only to make more room in our life for the Lord and receive the grace he pours out on us through the Holy Spirit. In other words, we fast in order to strengthen our faith. Jesus himself said as much! Once, when critics objected that his disciples didn't fast, Jesus explained that they would fast, not while he was present to them in person, but only after he had gone away (see Mk 2:19). These words can help us understand that Jesus invites us to fast today, in his absence, to make him more present to us now, so he might truly be at the center of our lives.

How? Because fasting can help us regain a proper perspective about food. Food can easily become an addiction. Many of us eat certain foods to make us feel better—we call them "comfort foods"—because they stimulate those brain circuits associated with pleasure and emotional well-being. The danger arises when the comfort becomes a compulsion. When that happens, we'll find ourselves thinking about food all the time or, ironically, eating without even thinking. Fasting can help us kick the habit. Not just because fasting suppresses insulin secretion, which decreases our taste for sugar. But also because it helps us to say "No!" to something we may not have said "No" to for a long time.

Fasting can also help us enjoy our food more. It's easy to take food for granted. We reach out for it, and it's there. Supermarkets, fast food establishments, and vending machines are everywhere we turn, and the food thrown away every day in our country could feed millions of people. We eat convenience foods "on the run," making sit-down meals a thing of the past. Fasting, however, can help us savor food more and gratefully treasure it as God's gift. To paraphrase Archbishop Fulton Sheen, we can either always be feasting and have a headache the next day, or observe times of fasting to make the feast even richer.[1]

Seen in this light, we can appreciate that fasting may be extended to far more than just food. In its fullest sense, fasting is a discipline through which we seek to detach ourselves from all the habits, preoccupations, compulsions, and addictions that can so easily clutter and contaminate our lives.

In and of themselves, some of these activities are harmless and at times even good—things like watching sports, reading the news, surfing the Internet, exercising, cooking, shopping, listening to music, or any other hobby or form of entertainment we might enjoy. Other compulsions are more obviously dangerous—things like excessive work, smoking and alcohol consumption, misused sexuality, and uncontrolled gambling.

Because they can become such a dominant force in our lives, activities such as these restrict our freedom to choose what is right. At their worst, they diminish our humanity by making us into their slaves. By fasting from them, however, we learn to say "No" to these destructive life patterns and can begin to break their hold upon us. By giving them less space in our lives, we create more space for God. And when God is given greater space in our life, the result is always joy. Fasting, then, even though it's an effort in self-denial, is also an act of affirming God. Fasting does involve saying "No," but it's a "No" that ultimately teaches us to say "Yes"—yes to God.

When Jesus was challenged about his disciples not fasting while he was with them, he responded by calling himself a bridegroom, and by referring to us, his friends, as guests at his wedding banquet. We might say, then, that we fast in order to feast: not on the things of this world, which are passing away, but on Jesus Christ—our life, our hope, and our joy.

Whenever we do it, it might be nice to know that fasting is now fashionable. And in the process, we might even shed a few pounds or kick a nagging habit! But best of all, we'll discover that by emptying our lives of one thing, God can fill the void with his love and deepen our faith.

 Chapter 24

# Take a Trip

It was a senior year rite of passage: all of us preparing to graduate from our high school had to memorize, and then recite, a portion of the Prologue from Geoffrey Chaucer's *Canterbury Tales*—in medieval English, no less, which is strikingly different from the language we speak today. Yet we all managed to muddle through it, and it's amazing how much I and some of my classmates have retained so many years later. One line, in particular, has always remained with me: "Than longen folk to goon on pilgrimages."[1]

As reflected in this literary masterpiece, religious pilgrimages were highly popular in the Middle Ages, and hostels and monasteries were happy to house pilgrims along the way. Like Chaucer's characters, some would travel to the great cathedral in Canterbury, England, to pray at the shrine of Saint Thomas Becket, who was martyred at an altar there. Rome was a popular destination too, as was Spain's Cathedral of Santiago de Compostela, where tradition holds that Saint James, a disciple of Jesus, is buried. To follow in the footsteps of Jesus, some, like Saint Francis of Assisi, made their way to the Holy Land. And for those who had neither the time nor the money for such an undertaking, there were any number of local shrines that could be visited—ordinary places made extraordinary by the presence of God.

But religious pilgrimages are by no means unique to the Middle Ages! The Bible's Old Testament speaks of devout Jews who would journey to Jerusalem to pray at the great Temple on Mount Zion. Along the way, they prayed the "Pilgrimage Psalms" (see Ps 120–134) that speak of God's protection and their longing to reach their destination: "I rejoiced when they said to me, 'Let us go to the house of the LORD'" (Ps 122:1). The Holy Family—Jesus, Mary, and Joseph—made this very pilgrimage each year. When Jesus was twelve, he remained behind in the Temple and impressed the teachers there with his wisdom—an event we Catholics recall in one of the joyful mysteries of the rosary.

Jesus himself was a traveler. We see this especially in Luke's Gospel and its companion volume, the Acts of the Apostles, which often present Jesus, his family, and his followers as being on a journey, a pilgrimage. For instance, his parents trekked from Nazareth to Bethlehem, where he was born and they were visited by the Magi, the "Three Kings," who had journeyed from far in the East to visit the new infant king. Jesus was born in a manger, as there was no room in the inn. And while popular tradition blames this on a heartless innkeeper, it may be that the inn, a lodging for travelers, signifies that Jesus, on earth, was simply passing through—having been sent by God the Father, and then returning to him.

In describing his ministry, Luke's Gospel highlights the journey of Jesus from Galilee to Jerusalem (see Lk 9:51–19:44). Along the way, Jesus encounters both blessings and hardships, as well as hospitality and hostility, but he always presses on in obedience to the Father's will. This journey would ultimately lead to his suffering and death. But it also resulted in his resurrection and ascension.

Saint Luke himself was a traveler; he accompanied Saint Paul on some of his lengthy missionary trips. Given this, perhaps it's not surprising that he made a point, more than the other Gospel writers, of recalling the journeys of Jesus and those who loved him. Yet he seems to have a deeper message here too, which is that, in imitation of Jesus, the Christian's life is a like a journey with the Lord. As did Jesus, we may have crosses to carry, but Jesus will never leave our side. Perhaps it's for this reason that the first title Luke uses to describe the Church is "The Way," and why he recalls how, on the first Easter, Jesus appeared to two unnamed disciples along the road to the village of Emmaus. As they walked together, their hearts burned as Jesus explained the Scriptures to them, and they recognized Jesus for who he is in "the breaking of the bread"—the sacrament of the Eucharist.

Since that Gospel was written, the life of faith has often been described as a journey of some sort. Along with many others, Saint Bernard of Clairvaux spoke of our faith journey as a ladder with God at the top, encouraging and supporting us as we make our way up, rung by rung. Saint John of the Cross spoke of our faith life as mountain trek—the "Ascent of Mount

Carmel"—as did Thomas Merton, who wrote of a "Seven Storey Mountain."[2] And as has been observed by many, we're never standing still in our spiritual life: we're either moving forward or sliding backward.

To find strength on our faith journey, we can take physical journeys—pilgrimages—on which we can find inspiration, challenge, and renewal. While our faith assures us that God is present everywhere, and at every time, a pilgrimage to a place associated with God's action in the past, with those who loved and served him in a heroic way, or simply designated as reserved for worship and prayer, can remind us that God is indeed always with us, even when we may wonder that he is not.

A pilgrimage isn't a vacation, although we can make a pilgrimage while on vacation. It's an opportunity to pray, reflect, and receive the sacraments. We can go alone or with a group; and we can go halfway around the world or to our diocese's shrine on the other side of town. But regardless of how far we go or with whom, our pilgrimage can remind us that we are but wayfarers on this earth, because our true home is heaven: "For here we have no lasting city" (Heb 13:14), as Scripture reminds us.

"It's not the destination, it's the journey" is a popular phrase often heard today. It means, I think, that sometimes we need to stop and smell the roses. And that's fine! But for the Christian, it is the destination: an eternity of joy with God in heaven. That's where we hope our life's pilgrimage will end, yet a pilgrimage or two here can certainly strengthen our fragile faith on the way.

# Part 3

# *Practical Things to Do*

 CHAPTER 25

# Be a Homebody

Carlo Carretto had spent twelve years living as a hermit in the Sahara Desert. With only the Blessed Sacrament for company, he lived alone, praying for long hours by himself, and translating the Bible into the language of the local nomads. For food, he milked a goat. But when he returned to his native Italy to visit his mother, Carlo Carretto came to the startling realization that she was far holier than he was. She was no hermit, and she didn't have much time for private prayer. Indeed, for thirty years she had been so busy with raising a family that she rarely had a private moment to herself. Nevertheless, the generosity and sacrifice of her motherhood had made her into a saint. Her holiness was learned at home.

Like Carlo Carretto did, we sometimes assume that we need to "get away from it all" to be with God. We think of our daily lives as obstacles to, and not opportunities for, growth in faith. But nothing could be farther from the truth! Holiness isn't reserved for hermits. All of us can become holy, whatever our circumstances. And for many of us—like Carlo Carretto's mother—those circumstances are centered upon our families. It's within the context of family relationships that God invites us to learn how to love, which is at the heart of holiness.

Families can provide the atmosphere in which we learn to relate to others: to care, to share, to love, and to forgive. That's one reason why Jesus insisted that a husband and wife become "one body" (Gn 2:24). This refers to much more than a physical union. Instead, it's a call to an intimate bond of two persons that requires personal change, self-giving, honest communication, openness to new life, forgiveness, patience, compassion, a desire to meet one another's needs, heal each other's hurts, and help each other become the person God intended him or her to be.

Forming such a union requires both commitment and sacrifice, but through that effort, we will catch glimmers of God's perfect, unconditional love, and appreciate the sacrifice Jesus made for our salvation. Those with children can also glimpse God's love through the love they share with them. When their children make mistakes or go astray, the parents experience something of God's heartbreak when we turn away from him. As parents watch their children grow and mature, they taste something of God's joy when he sees us advance in holiness. It's been said that God is pleased with our hesitant, wavering steps in faith, much as a parent delights in the first, uncertain steps of a toddler. Parents also come to appreciate God's boundless patience with us as they try, however imperfectly, to exercise patience with their sons and daughters.

It's for these reasons that the family is understood as a school of love. Love is God's gift, but it's also an art learned through observation and experience. And there is no better place to learn it than at home. It's in the home that children can learn that they're loved and accepted—knowledge that forms the basis of their self-image, their relationships with other people, and their relationship with God. And in the process, as the *Catechism of the Catholic Church* reminds us, "Children in turn contribute to the *growth in holiness* of their parents" (CCC no. 2227). As one expert put it, parents are good not because of what their children become. Parents are good because of what they become in the process.

In their role as teachers of love, parents are never "off duty." Everything they do and say rubs off on their children—for good and for bad. The way they speak, the way they treat others, the way they cope with disagreements, the way they show compassion and forgiveness are all vitally important. Indeed, how parents behave critically shapes a child's image of God—a process that begins with the tiniest of babies. For instance, when a parent picks up a crying baby, the baby learns that when he or she cries out, somebody cares and listens—a valuable first lesson in prayer. Playing peek-a-boo helps a child understand that Mommy or Daddy is there even when he or she can't be seen. At the same time, this can help a child appreciate later that God is always with us, even though he can't be seen. Paying attention to children and spending time with them says that they're valuable and lovable—essential knowledge for mature faith, fruitful relationships, and good mental health.

Indeed, time is one of the most precious gifts we can give to someone we love. We show how important someone is to us by the time we invest in them. That's why family relationships should get the best of our time and be a number-one priority, in spite of our busy schedules. So sit around the dinner table!

Linger over coffee. Play catch outside or games on the floor. Drop that note or make that phone call. Visit Mom on Mother's Day. Focus on each other, instead of a screen. Above all, sharing faith within the family is always time well spent. Indeed, parents are four times more effective than clergy, and ten times more effective than teachers, in passing on the faith to children.

Blessed Teresa of Calcutta was once asked, "Mother Teresa, you've done so much to make the world a better place. What can we do?" She answered with a smile: "Love your children as much as you can. Love your children so they *know* you love them. That is best." Although this comment was directed to parents, her words echo the wise advice I was given years ago: "Never underestimate the spiritual value of family life." That principle holds true regardless of the state of our family, and whether we're married or not. Any family can become a school of love because, as Scripture reminds us, "Whoever loves is a child of God and loves God."[1]

 CHAPTER 26

# Get a Job

Not many best-selling songs have been written about people who love their jobs. Instead, popular songs about work are usually concerned with either avoiding it or enduring it because it's such a grind and a drudgery. Singers gripe about the dreariness of the "9 to 5" routine and how they work only for "the weekend." Some would rather bang on a drum than work; others want to tell their bosses where they can "shove" their lousy jobs. Such sentiments seem to echo the curse given to Adam when he was banished from the Garden of Eden, and how he would struggle to eat only "by the sweat of your face" (Gn 3:19).

Thankfully, our faith paints a far more attractive picture of work. After all, God himself works! His creating heaven and earth is described as "work," after which he rests and proclaims all he has made to be "good." Jesus certainly worked, too, as a carpenter like Saint Joseph, his foster father. And in his teaching, "Jesus constantly proclaims the kingdom of God through the lens of the human worker: the shepherd, farmer, sower, homemaker, servant, steward, fisherman, merchant, and laborer."[1]

Work, then, although exhausting and frustrating at times, can also be God-like and good. It doesn't have to be something that breaks our spirits. Instead, our work can be an expression of our faith and can even strengthen it. Indeed, we can treasure it as a gift from God. After all, our work generates needed income for us and for our families, and it offers goods and services that benefit others. It provides opportunities to enjoy meaningful relationships, enhance our culture, develop society, and transform the environment. Through using and developing our gifts and skills, we can become better people. Work also allows us to complete and perfect God's work of creation. Just as Adam was called upon to care for and cultivate the Garden of Eden, we by our work can help make the world a more beautiful and hospitable place.

We're invited to offer our work to God at each and every Mass. During the preparation of the gifts, the bread is described as that which "human hands have made," and the wine is identified as "the work of human hands." These gifts represent all our labor, offered with gratitude and love. God takes them, transforms them, and gives them back to us as the Body and Blood of his Son. In this wonderful exchange of gifts, God accepts our work and incorporates it into his work of making us holy.

Because work is at the same time God's gift to us and our gift to God, all honest work is meaningful and dignified and may be undertaken with pride. This is especially important to remember in our culture, in which the value of one's work is often measured by the size of one's paycheck. Yet consider Jesus' work as a carpenter. In his day, to be a carpenter meant that one's family had lost their ancestral plot of land. It wasn't lucrative work by any means, and most carpenters barely eked out a living. Yet Jesus, the eternally begotten Son of God, King of kings and Lord of lords, didn't think it beneath his dignity to engage in this type of work.

Not all work, however, is acceptable for a Christian. As followers of Jesus we should be sensitive to the impact our work, or our employers' products and practices, is having on its clients and customers. In other words, the work we do should be compatible with the values we profess. We might ask ourselves: Does our work promote or stimulate morally harmful desires, like greed or addiction? Does it foster injustices, like sweat shop labor? Is it honest and forthright in its practices and public representation? If the answer to any of these questions is "No," a Christian has two choices: try to change the situation, or consider changing jobs.

Our faith and our work should walk hand in hand. When Jesus invited Saint Matthew to become an apostle, he did so by entering his workplace—in his case, a tax office—and saying "Follow me" (Mt 9:9). Jesus invites us to follow him in the workplace too, and not leave our faith at home as we walk out the door. Think of it this way: At Sunday Mass we gather in community "with bread," or in Latin, *cum pane*. On Monday we go to the "company," the place of our work, where we can bring the Spirit of our Sunday "com-panionship."

Allowing our faith *to* work, while we're *at* work, creates an opportunity to transform our workplace through love, joy, peace, patience, kindness, generosity, faithfulness, gentleness, and self-control. As Bishop Michael Saltarelli once wrote, "By conducting ourselves always as disciples of Christ, we preach the Gospel through our very presence on the job."[2]

We also bring faith into the workplace by upholding human dignity and opposing injustice. We must choose to treat others with fairness and stand in solidarity with those who are being hurt through racism, sexual harassment, age discrimination, false rumors, and unjust wages and work conditions. And we need to be honest, too, as *dis*honesty is rampant in the work world today. As Christians, we're called to swim against this tide. "If you are honest and frank," Blessed Teresa of Calcutta is said to have written, "people may cheat you. Be honest and frank anyway."

The bottom line is that while work is meant to be a part of our lives, work is not our reason for living. Jesus Christ is our reason for living. He calls us to work, but he calls us to work in a Christ-like way. As Christians, we don't pursue holiness in *spite* of our work. It is precisely *through* our work that we are challenged to grow in holiness and build up God's kingdom.[3] This is true when we find our work meaningful and satisfying, and it's true when our work generates difficulties and anxieties. Either way, our faith will enhance our work. "How do I prove my love for God?" asked Blessed Teresa. "By doing beautifully the work I have been given to do."[4]

# Lighten Your Load

Istanbul, Turkey, like so many of the world's largest cities, is rife with slums and poverty. Yet, along the shores of the Bosporus, dividing Asia from Europe, may be found the waterside homes of Istanbul's rich and famous. One such resident was interviewed for *National Geographic*. This person and her late husband were art collectors, and she was most proud of the treasures they had amassed over the years—silver, porcelains, and especially paintings. Their collection, she boasted, included a Tintoretto, a small Rembrandt, and two Titians. But in spite of her wealth, this woman was far from happy. "Too many things," she sighed. "They require much care. I am their slave."[1]

Many of us—whether or not we're actually rich—understand exactly where she's coming from. Having spent so much time and energy in the pursuit of the material and the worldly, we find ourselves jaded and exhausted—burdened with stuff or the desire for it, perhaps saddled with debt, and left with an emptiness inside that there must be something more to life than just this. The truth is, God created the things of this world to be at *our* service. Yet, as the woman in Istanbul discovered, they can lay such a claim on our energies and desires that we are actually at *their* service. That's why our Lord stressed so strongly the necessity of simple living.

Yet living simply can be such a challenge because possessions and wealth can play deeply symbolic roles in our lives, representing different things to different people. For instance, money can be a substitute for love, as seen in those who lavish their spouses or children with gifts instead of time or affection. To some, money is power because it can buy influence and access and serve as a tool for persuasion, manipulation, and coercion. For others, money is security and safety, blanketing a fear of debt, bankruptcy, and destitution. Also, money is frequently equated with self-esteem, self-worth, or a sense of independence. As one marriage counselor explains, "If money were just money, everyone would make rational decisions about it. But it's not. It's very emotionally loaded."[2]

Worst of all, as Jesus warns us, money and possessions can displace God from his rightful place in our lives and lead us to turn our backs on him. "No one can serve two masters," he explained. "You cannot serve God and mammon" (Mt 6:24).[3] When money and possessions become a dominant force in our lives, one of two things will happen: If we don't have them, we'll become envious of those who do, and we may even come to resent God. Or, when we do have them, we'll just forget about God altogether. When money equals security and self-worth, God becomes irrelevant. Perhaps it's for good reason that our U.S. currency has to remind us "In God We Trust!"

Jesus did not say that money and the things of this world are evil. Jesus himself used money, and he taught that God made everything in creation good and has given them to us for our use and enjoyment. Furthermore, Jesus never said that it's a sin to be rich. At the same time, he pulled no punches when he warned that it is easier for a camel to pass through a needle's eye than for one who is rich to enter God's kingdom. He knows that riches can so easily give rise to greed and pride, blind us to what is truly important in life, and absorb far too much of our time, energy, and thoughts. And this is where the sin lies. As English philosopher Francis Bacon purportedly observed, "Money is a good servant, but a poor master."

But how might money be a servant instead of a master? Mother Teresa answered this question by proposing that money is useful only if it helps to spread the love of God.[4] That may sound rather "pie in the sky," especially when we're paying our utility bills! But in reality, it's a very practical outlook that can radically shape our every purchase or financial decision. It leads us to ask questions like, "Why are we doing this?" "What purpose will this serve?" "What would Jesus do?" or "Will this help build the kingdom of God?"

How we answer these questions will vary and depend on our needs and circumstances. Our answers will certainly challenge us to reconsider our attitudes toward money, our motives when using money, the distinction between our wants and our needs, and how what we have might help meet the needs of others. Our answers won't necessarily require us to live Spartan, colorless lives! But hopefully they'll lead us to use our money and possessions in a way that is pleasing to the Lord, which will strengthen our faith and replace greed with generosity and gratitude. At the very least, they can prevent us, as is popularly said, from buying things we don't want, with money we don't have, to impress people we don't even like!

Cardinal Theodore McCarrick tells the story of two men who were walking along a busy New York City street one afternoon. One turned to his companion and exclaimed, "Did you hear that beautiful bird?" "Are you kidding?" came the reply. "Who on earth could hear a bird over all this racket?" But just then, somebody dropped their pocket change on the sidewalk—and everybody came to a screeching halt.

The point here is that in our noisy culture it can be easier to hear the alluring call of money than it is to hear the usually gentle voice of God, whose words get drowned out like the songbird. When that happens, "almighty God" gets displaced by the "almighty dollar." That's why God invites us to lighten our load and live more simply so that our faith may flourish. We need not, like the woman in Istanbul, feel enslaved by stuff. Because, as is celebrated in *Simple Gifts*, a beloved American hymn, "'Tis the gift to be simple, 'tis the gift to be free."[5]

 CHAPTER 28

# Kick the Habit

At age twelve Matt Talbot began drinking. Most men in his large family were heavy drinkers, and Matt's first jobs in a wine shop and with whiskey shipments at the Dublin docks provided plenty of temptations. For the next fifteen years, Matt was a chronic alcoholic. One night, however, penniless and desperate, Matt made a pledge not to drink again. And until he died forty years later, he never had another drop of booze. For strength, he turned to God, attending Mass daily and spending long hours in prayer. Matt died in obscurity, but today his grave is visited each year by thousands who are inspired by his victory over alcoholism. In 1975 the Church declared him "venerable"—the first step in the process toward sainthood.

Like Matt Talbot, many people wrestle with alcoholism. Yet even if alcohol isn't a problem for us, there's likely something in our life to which we have an addiction, a compulsion, or, at the very least, an unhealthy attachment. We can become addicted to all sorts of things: work, exercise, shopping, the Internet and social media, reading, promoting a cause, fame and reputation, playing the stock market, winning, hobbies, pornography, following the news, gossiping, socializing, junk food, TV shows, sex, caffeine, tobacco, and so on. As a priest friend of mine once said, only half-jokingly: "We all have at least ten addictions. If we say we don't, we're addicted to lying!"

There's nothing funny, however, about addictions. They can preoccupy us at best and destroy us at worst. We can become anxious and irritable when we don't get our fix, straining our relationships and work performance. In serious cases, we may experience more severe withdrawal symptoms. Not surprisingly, our relationship with God suffers too. Years ago I heard it said that unchecked habits and compulsions are some of the greatest obstacles to advancing in the spiritual life. And how true that is!

An easy way to identify our addictions is to consider our thoughts and feelings. We can ask ourselves: What preoccupies our minds? What makes us upset? What cheers us up? What causes anger or disappointment? What stresses us out? What drives us or makes us anxious? In other words, as Catholic psychologist Robert Wicks has written, "What is blackmailing us into believing something must result or someone must respond in a certain way before we can be at peace, joyful?"[1]

Freedom from addictions, compulsions, and bad habits is essential for our growth in faith. Because when we're freed from those things that control us, we have more space in our life for God to be in control. We can't become free on our own, however. Willpower isn't enough. What we can do is open these corners of our life to God's healing and mercy and allow his grace to do what we ourselves cannot.

The first step toward freedom is to admit that we have a problem. This can be a challenge because we can become very comfortable with our habits. Sometimes we make excuses such as, "Everybody's doing it" or "Nobody's perfect" or "I deserve a little fun every now and then" or "At least I'm not as bad as the next guy" or "The ends justify the means" or even "Doesn't God want me to be happy?" We need to get beyond our excuses to get beyond our problem.

The next thing we can do is strictly avoid what Catholics have traditionally called the "near occasions of sin"—those places, persons, or circumstances that trigger a temptation in us. Matt Talbot, for instance, would cross a street rather than walk in front of a bar knowing that its sights, sounds, and smells would tempt him to drink. Like him, we do well to steer clear of problem situations. And if it's impossible to avoid them, then we at least need to fortify ourselves with prayer beforehand when we know they're coming.

Indeed, prayer is essential when kicking the habit—prayer for strength, prayer for healing, prayer for inner peace. "He who does not give up prayer," promised Saint Alphonsus Liguori, "cannot continue to habitually offend God." Regular Mass—even daily—is a help too. As Matt Talbot learned, God strengthens us against temptation through the grace of the Eucharist. Saint Bernard observed that when our urges to self-indulgence weaken, we are experiencing the power of that sacrament at work.

Confession is another essential sacrament for our struggle. In confession, not only are we forgiven for the things we've done, we also take responsibility for them. We admit, "*I* did this" or "*I* did that," instead of making excuses, ignoring our behavior, or blaming our circumstances. By taking ownership of our habit, we'll take it more seriously. And when we take it more seriously, we'll fight it more seriously.

In addition to confessing to God, we can also reveal our struggles to a friend, counselor, or support group, who can offer us encouragement and wisdom and hold us accountable. So often we keep our habits a secret because we're ashamed of them. The truth is millions of people face the same struggles we do, and we can find great strength when we face struggles together.

Finally, it's always good to recall that since habits weren't formed overnight, they won't be kicked overnight. It's best to take things one day at a time and try to relax—because reducing stress can reduce temptation. Instead of being anxious, we can "let go and let God," as a popular slogan puts it. We should be as patient with ourselves as God is with us. Sometimes we aren't, and we become discouraged when our habits persist. But that's the last thing our Lord wants us to do, because when we get discouraged, we lose hope. And when we lose hope, we throw in the towel and give up the struggle. It's better to take the advice of Saint Mary Margaret Alacoque: "Keep your heart in peace, and let nothing trouble you, not even your faults. You must humble yourself and amend them peacefully, without becoming discouraged or cast down, because God's dwelling is in peace."

 CHAPTER 29

# Get Help from Your Friends

After purchasing a house at a sheriff's auction, a Toledo, Ohio, man was understandably excited to move into his new home. When he finally did, however, he was horrified to discover the remains of the previous inhabitant, who had been dead for some time. Apparently, no one had noticed that he was missing or had gone looking for him.[1]

This tragic incident is sadly reflective of our increasingly impersonal society, in which genuine human contact is harder and harder to come by. Such isolation takes its toll. Studies have shown that the fewer human connections we have at home, at work, in the community, and in religious institutions, the more likely we are to get sick, be filled with anxiety, and die prematurely. Conversely, these same studies indicate that the *more* human connections we have, the more likely we are to enjoy a long and healthy life.

We weren't made to live alone. "No man is an island," as the poet John Donne reminds us.[2] We are made instead for relationships because we have been created in the image of God the Holy Trinity—a communion of three Persons: Father, Son, and Holy Spirit—who share one divine life of perfect, boundless love. It follows, then, that we flourish and prosper when nurtured within loving relationships. As Blessed Pope John Paul II has written: "Human beings are not made for solitude . . . they grow to the extent that they enter into relationships with others. They need *interpersonal relationships* that are rich in inner depth, gratuitousness, and self-sacrifice."[3]

Friendships are some of the most important relationships we can have. Jesus himself had many friends. During his earthly ministry, he surrounded himself with disciples and other companions—both men and women. Jesus seeks friendship with us too.

Our human friendships can help us to understand and accept Jesus' offer, as was learned by a woman I know well. Although both talented and beautiful, she is very different from her family, who never really understood her. This knowledge was both painful and frustrating for her, and she never really felt loved and accepted by them for who she is. She felt that they always wanted her to be somebody different, somebody else. She wondered if God thought the same way.

But then someone came into her life who was able to read her like a book and who knew right away what made her tick. This experience of being understood and accepted was a real turning point in her life. She began to feel lovable, empowered, confident, hopeful, and joyful. And she began to realize, maybe for the first time in her life, that Jesus really loved her. She was able to accept Jesus' acceptance of her because she had been accepted by somebody else.

The love of friends, then, can open our eyes to the love of God. Friends can also open our eyes to God's will, as Saint Francis of Assisi once learned. Early in life, he found himself at a crossroads. On the one hand, he thought that perhaps God was calling him to a quiet life of prayer and contemplation. On the other hand, he wondered if God wanted him to be a traveling missionary and preacher of the Gospel. To help decide, he turned to two friends—Saint Clare and Brother Sylvester—whom he asked to pray for him and get back to him. They prayed and then sent a messenger to Saint Francis. When the messenger arrived, Saint Francis asked, "What has my Lord Jesus Christ commanded that I should do?" "That thou go throughout the world to preach," came the reply. Upon hearing these words, Saint Francis jumped up and exclaimed: "Let us be going in the name of God!"[4]

Friends can also challenge us when we fail to live in God's will, as we all sometimes do. On our own, we can be blind to our faults and shortcomings. As Saint John Climacus observed, "God has arranged that no one can see his own faults as clearly as his neighbor does."[5] That's why God invites friends to correct each other—so they can build each other up in love.

God can speak to us through other people; we can hear the voice of Christ through the voices of our friends. And should our friends challenge us, it would be wise for us to listen, because they might be acting as the very mouthpiece of the Holy Spirit. And when that happens, we should be grateful instead of defensive and humble instead of proud. Pride says, "There's nothing wrong with me!" But humility says, "I'm still a work in progress."

Speaking though our friends, Jesus can say: "Be open to challenge; be receptive to constructive criticism; don't resist charitable correction!" Acceptance of criticism says to God that we're open to grow. And when we're open to grow, God can fill us with his grace.

Different friends can be a blessing to us in different ways. Catholic author Robert Wicks proposes that we need four distinct types of people in our lives: First, we need "prophets" who ask the question: "What guides and shapes the decisions you make?" Second, we require "cheerleaders" who support us when the going gets rough. Third, "harassers" are necessary to tease us so we don't take ourselves too seriously. Fourth, we need "spiritual guides" who encourage us to find meaning in our lives.[6] In short, we need people who love us, support us, guide us, challenge us, and make us laugh. We need people with whom we can share our sorrows and our joys, reveal our dreams and heartaches, and express our honest feelings. We need other people in order to be fully human.

And to be fully human is to reflect the God in whose image we are made—a God of relationships, a God of love. Indeed, "God is friendship," observed Saint Aelred of Rievaulx. And true human friendships can help us to live in friendship with the Lord. That's why Saint Thomas Aquinas could conclude: "There is nothing on this earth more to be prized than true friendship."

## CHAPTER 30

# Count Your Blessings

We often ask people "How are you?" when we greet them; normally, it follows "Hi" or "Hey" or "Hello" as in "Hi, how are you?" When we ask this question, we're usually just trying to be friendly and pleasant; we really don't expect to hear about how the other person is honestly doing. Most people understand this, and it's reflected in the way they respond. They'll say things like "Fine" or "I'm okay" or "Busy" or "Thank God, it's Friday," or something along those lines.

However, not everyone replies with one of the typical, stock responses. One colleague of mine always made me smile whenever I greeted her in the hallways. I'd see her and say, "Hi Margaret, how are you?" and nine times out of ten she'd stop in her tracks, stand up straight, and say, "I am absolutely wonderful!"

Margaret is not alone. There are those who, when greeted, will respond with a cheerful, "Best day of my life!" or "Never been better!" or "I'm great!" or, especially in the African-American community, "I'm blessed!" Those who say such things are, from my experience, fundamentally grateful people. They are thankful for what they have and who they are, and they can't help but express it. They're typically a joy to be around! They are also few and far between.

An incident from Jesus' ministry challenges us to grow in gratitude (see Lk 17:11–19). As he entered a village, ten people with leprosy, a dreaded disease in his day, cried out to Jesus, pleading for help. After Jesus cured them, they ran off toward Jerusalem to present themselves to the Jewish priests, who could certify that they'd been healed and allow them to rejoin their communities. One of the lepers stopped in his tracks and returned to thank Jesus. The others, however, did not, much to Jesus' dismay. "Where are the other nine?" (Lk 17:17) he wondered, expressing his disappointment at their lack of gratitude.

Like those nine, all of us, at times, might benefit from growth in gratitude. The good news is that being grateful is beneficial, as various studies have demonstrated. One experiment had a group of young adults make a daily record of things they were thankful for, while another group of young adults made lists of headaches and hassles. After three weeks, those who counted blessings reported feeling more energetic and optimistic than the others, and they slept better as well. Furthermore, those in the group that counted blessings were more likely to reach out and help those with personal problems and offer support. This suggests that while ingratitude can breed selfishness, gratitude inspires service. In addition, this and other studies have shown that grateful people are, overall, healthier and happier. As G. K. Chesterton concluded, "The test of all happiness is gratitude."[1]

Perhaps gratitude's greatest benefit is that it opens our eyes to goodness and kindness in our world—things we might otherwise be blind to or take for granted. And, when we recognize that all these blessings, however small, come from the hand of God and are signs of his love and care for us, we come to know how present God is to us, and our faith will grow. That's why, when our faith feels fragile, it's good to make an intentional effort to count our blessings. In other words, cultivating gratitude can cultivate a stronger faith.

And gratitude does need to be cultivated! Gratitude is not something we're born with but rather something we need to learn. Parents have to teach and remind their children to say the magic words "Please" and "Thank you." However, our apprenticeship in gratitude should continue through adulthood because we inhabit a consumer culture that reminds us, all the time, of everything we *don't* have. It can tempt us to live beyond our means, confuse our needs with our wants, be envious of what others may have, and conclude that we're entitled to them. That's why it's a good practice to regularly count our blessings and make an intentional effort to call to mind all the things for which we should be grateful.

"In all circumstances give thanks," Saint Paul encourages us, "for this is the will of God for you in Christ Jesus" (1 Thes 5:18). Should we take his advice, we'll discover much in our lives to be grateful for—even during the most challenging of times. We can give thanks for the littlest of things: a morning cup of coffee, the fact that the toilet flushed, a smile from a stranger. In our nation, we can be grateful for things we enjoy that those who live elsewhere do not, such as clean drinking water, freedoms of speech and religion, democracy, and access to education and health care. With grace and time, we might be able to accept difficult and painful things as blessings because we'll come to see them as opportunities God gave us to grow in patience and love. Most of all, God invites us to be grateful for his greatest gifts to us—mercy, redemption, forgiveness, the gift of the Holy Spirit, hope of life everlasting, and the knowledge that this world, with its pain and brokenness, is passing away, to be replaced by a perfect existence filled with peace and joy, where tears are not shed and relationships are healed.

As Christians, gratitude involves more than simply being thankful for our blessings. It also involves expressing our thanks to the source of our blessings, God himself. One way we can do this is by sharing our blessings through giving and service, so they might bless others as well. In addition, it's for good reason that our central act of worship is called the "Eucharist," which in Greek means "thanksgiving." At the Eucharist, we are able to bring our gratitude to the altar and offer it to God as an act of praise, in the beautiful words of Psalm 145:10: "All your works give you thanks, O LORD, and your faithful bless you."

 CHAPTER 31

# Do the Dishes

*The Journal of Mundane Behavior* was a scholarly journal featuring articles that considered the ordinary and routine activities and experiences that fill our days. Its issues explored the significance of shaving, running errands, the table arrangement and background noise of a neighborhood café, and the making of a peanut butter and jelly sandwich. One cover featured a photograph of a man standing in his backyard with a pooper-scooper. The sociologist who created this journal did so because he was concerned that his professional colleagues were so preoccupied with the extreme and the unusual that they virtually ignored the day-to-day stuff that fills most people's lives.[1]

The same might be said, at times, about our attitudes toward our faith and our approach toward our religion. We can give so much attention and ascribe such great importance to the exceptional and the extraordinary, while that which is seemingly small, trivial, and routine is written off as insignificant or unimportant. We can be awed by accounts of miracles and admire those who make heroic sacrifices—as we should! At the same time, we can fail to appreciate the importance of daily discipline, quiet perseverance, and honoring one's responsibilities.

Jesus, however, knows full well the value of such things. He once told a parable in which certain servants were praised precisely because they had been "faithful in small matters" (see Mt 25:14–30). Through this story, Jesus stresses that when it comes to our journey with him, little things can mean a lot. Small, unnoticed acts of faith, kindness, and generosity, and fidelity to our daily routines and duties are essential for our spiritual growth and are deeply important in his eyes. Yet this is a truth we can easily forget, immersed as we are in a culture that prizes public recognition and the grand gesture.

Because our Lord values "small matters," we can hope to encounter him in them and trust that doing them honors him in some way. However, even the most religious of people can fail to grasp this, as was learned by Catholic writer Ronald Rolheiser in a seminar he attended on prayer. At one point, the seminar's facilitator described her own prayer life, which was centered upon meditating in silence for two hours each day. She claimed that this practice has resulted in some very moving experiences of God.

Rolheiser asked her how these experiences of God during meditation compared with the experiences she had through her ordinary, day-to-day routines of home and work. In response, she readily confessed that she didn't expect to encounter God there at all. She went on to insist that one shouldn't confuse "religious" experience with what she called "human" experience.[2]

Like her, we too can make a disconnect between "religion" and "everyday life." In so doing, we can easily forget that God is present at all times and in all places, including in the midst of our daily routines. As a consequence, we pass up many wonderful opportunities to encounter the Lord and grow in grace. As Jean-Pierre de Caussade, a seventeenth-century French Jesuit, once wrote, "You seek God and he is everywhere; everything proclaims him, everything gives him to you."[3]

But how do we do this? How might we encounter God through the seemingly dull, daily routines of life? How might mowing the lawn, cooking dinner, folding the laundry, cleaning the floors, waiting in line, or commuting to work become grace-filled moments? It's easy to dismiss these times as wasted, chores to be done, or "necessary evils" to be endured before we can move on to more exciting and more productive things.

An answer was provided for us three hundred years ago by a simple Carmelite monk, Brother Lawrence. In his classic little book, *The Practice of the Presence of God*, he explains that things we might be tempted to do grudgingly or reluctantly can be done cheerfully and joyfully if we do them for the glory and praise of God.

Can we really drive the carpool or pay our household bills for the glory of God? Yes! They are acts of service, and any act of service can glorify God if done in the right spirit. They're a way we can imitate Jesus, who came "not to be served but to serve" (Mt 20:28 *RSV*). All Jesus did he did with love, and he knows that anything we do with love can be a blessing to those around us. "Pick up a pin from a motive of love," explained Saint Thérèse of Lisieux, "and you may thereby convert a soul."[4] I recall how once I was preparing a homily on the value of doing routine things. As it happened, Stephanie, my wife, saw what I was writing just as she was going to wash the last of the Thanksgiving dinner dishes, and her attitude about that task changed dramatically. "I'm going to wash these dishes for God," she announced. And she did—with a vastly improved attitude!

When faced with the prospect of being faithful in "small matters," sometimes the world will tempt us into thinking that they don't matter because we don't matter. We're just not important enough. At other times, our pride will insist that we're too important to do them. Such things are beneath us. But God doesn't think we're unimportant, and he doesn't want us to be puffed up *by* pride. Instead, he wants us to do what we do *with* pride because what we do does matter. As Dr. Martin Luther King, Jr., reminded us, we can sweep a street like Raphael painted pictures, Michelangelo carved marble, and Shakespeare wrote poetry.[5]

There's no escaping the fact that our lives are filled with mundane tasks. But they need not be something to simply endure with clenched teeth! Because if we approach such tasks with a joyful heart and do these ordinary things extraordinarily well for God's glory, they can be true occasions of grace. Very rarely do we have opportunities to do great things for God. Yet every day presents us with many small things to do for God, who invites us to embrace them cheerfully. And should we be faithful in doing these small things, we may well find our faith becoming great.

## CHAPTER 32

# Apply the Brakes

Have you ever found yourself wishing for a big snowstorm that would shut everything down for a few days? Sure, snow can give rise to any number of headaches. But at the same time, snow days can force us into slowing our life's pace a little bit. When work, school, and activities are canceled (and possibly the Internet is down too), we receive a gift of time during which we can play board games, bake treats, reconnect with one another, curl up with a good book, and take a much needed "breather."

Taking breathers is not something we Americans are especially good at doing. Surveys reveal that we spend more time on the job than workers in almost every other nation. Our children's lives are typically overbooked as well, their days being filled with sports practices, music and dance lessons, club activities, and increasing amounts of homework.

All sorts of negative consequences can arise from our excessive activity. We become candidates for burnout and place ourselves at risk for stress and the related problems of eating disorders, headaches, high blood pressure, depression, drug and alcohol abuse—even suicide! We rob ourselves of opportunities to daydream, reflect, and have fun. Parents don't spend time enjoying their children and passing along their values and adult wisdom. Friends and spouses don't communicate with one another as they should. And we deprive ourselves of the sleep we need, making us crabby, less productive on the job, vulnerable to illness, and dangerous behind the wheel. Giraffes may sleep only thirty minutes a day. We, however, need at least seven or eight hours of restful sleep.

Excessive activity can compromise our spiritual life as well, as Jesus himself cautions us. "Beware that your hearts do not become drowsy," he warned, "from . . . the anxieties of daily life" (Lk 21:34). When he spoke these words, he was referring to his coming again in glory at the end of time. He didn't want his listeners to be so distracted and busy that they wouldn't be prepared to greet him when he came. But his words are intended for us too. He knows that frenzied activity can produce a flimsy faith, and he longs for us to recognize him when he comes into our lives today.

Jesus invites us to slow down, just as he encouraged his disciples to slow down. Once, the disciples had come back together after having been away on missionary journeys, and they surely must have been exhausted. We can also imagine that they wanted to swap tales and share their experiences with each other. Yet so many people were pressing in to speak with Jesus, and with them, that they couldn't find an opportunity to rest and reconnect. And so Jesus, recognizing the disciples' need, invited them to get away from the crowds and spend some time together in a deserted place (see Mk 6:30–32).

The challenge for us is this: If Jesus thought it important to rest and spend quality time with those he loved, shouldn't we do the same? In other words, if as Christians we are to live in imitation of Jesus, then we need to make time for family, friends, and refreshment. The earliest Christians knew this. Their leaders, such as Saint Augustine, emphasized the need for *Otium Sanctum*, Latin for "holy leisure," which we might understand as slowing down by stepping back from work, not in order to waste time, but use it to nourish our relationships with God and others.

We need "holy leisure" because we all can benefit from a measure of balance in our lives. In fact, this is such an important topic that our Church has stressed, in its *Pastoral Constitution on the Church in the Modern World*, that leisure is necessary to foster "familial, cultural, social, and religious life." Elsewhere, this same document hopes: "May this leisure be used properly to relax, to fortify the health of soul and body through spontaneous study and activity."[1] Understood this way, leisure time is not wasted time, a conclusion sometimes made in our productivity-obsessed world. Instead, leisure allows us to fulfill our need to spend time with ourselves, spend time with each other, and spend time with the Lord.

For the health of our bodies and souls, let's find time for leisure time. Let's gather around our tables and share our stories with each other. Let's open a book or watch a movie that might stretch our minds or soften our hearts. Let's exercise and get the blood really flowing through our veins. Take a good hard look at your commitments and obligations and consider cutting out a few things. Reach out and touch that person you've been meaning to call for so long. Stare at the clouds and dream dreams. Rediscover an old hobby or take up a new one. Play with your kids. Take a mental health day. Take a nap. Say a prayer.

Scripture shares that God himself rested after having created the heavens and the earth (Gn 2:2). In the Ten Commandments, God actually insists that we rest like he did, on the Sabbath day, which for us is Sunday. If we truly honored that, we'd enjoy the equivalent of nearly seven weeks of vacation each year!

It's claimed that psychologist Carl Jung concluded that hurry isn't of the devil—it *is* the devil. So if it's the devil we're looking for, by all means, let's speed things up! But if it's God we're seeking, then for heaven's sake, let's slow things down.

# Part 4

## *Fun Things to Do*

## CHAPTER 33

# Get Your Head in the Game

S aint Paul is a remarkable and complex character. He was a tentmaker and a scholar, and he established new churches all over the map. During his extensive travels to preach about Jesus, he was shipwrecked, beaten, and imprisoned. His letters reveal that he was a deeply passionate individual! They also suggest that he may have been a sports fan. When describing the life of faith, Saint Paul refers to running races, competing for medals, training to win, and even boxing. Given the times and places where he lived, he was certainly aware of the ancient Olympic games and was likely more familiar with the Isthmian Games, held every two years near the city of Corinth, which he knew well.[1]

Just as Saint Paul did, many people today use sports imagery to understand and teach the faith. A friend of mine learned this from a nun he sought out for spiritual guidance. "Good!"

she exclaimed, upon learning that he enjoys golfing. She explained that in golf, the concentration needed to hit the ball can also benefit one's prayer life by helping to keep one's mind from wandering and being filled with distracting thoughts, which are typical struggles in prayer.

Blessed John Paul II was personally convinced of the connections between faith and sports. He was sometimes called "God's athlete" because of his love for hiking, canoeing, and soccer, which he played as a goalie. As a boy he would even play soccer with his dad inside their home. He was especially fond of skiing and would occasionally sneak out of the Vatican to hit the slopes. Before he became pope, he once joked, with tongue in cheek, that it was unacceptable for a cardinal to be a poor skiier.[2] But on a more serious note, he would write at times about the spiritual benefits of sports. "Sport," he explained, "can communicate very profound values."[3]

Saint Paul highlighted some of those "profound values" in his writing. He stressed, for instance, the importance of good teamwork—both for athletes and followers of Jesus. In a letter to one church, whose members had been fighting, he begged them to start "working together" (see Phil 1:27–30), using the Greek words meaning, "playing together on the same team."[4] Teamwork, Saint Paul seems to be saying, is not only needed to compete well in sports, it's also essential for the Church to be one, united, loving family.

To help this conflicted community overcome its fears and have courage in the face of hostile adversaries, Saint Paul again turned to sports imagery. Don't be "intimidated in any way by your opponents" (Phil 1:28), he encouraged, using a motivational appeal familiar to any coach today. Elsewhere, he assured this same group that they don't face their challenges alone, because "we are all engaged on the same *agon*" (a Greek word for "athletic contest").[5]

Saint Paul drove home many other points through sports talk. Discipline, he said, is essential not only for improvement as an athlete but also to growth in faith,[6] because discipline leads to self-control, and self-control enables us to live in freedom from those negative habits that can lead us away from God. Yet discipline is not enough, according to Saint Paul. Obedience is also necessary for our faith life, just as playing by the rules is essential in sports. "[A]n athlete cannot receive the winner's crown," he wrote to his friend Saint Timothy, "except by competing according to the rules" (2 Tm 2:5).

Perseverance in faith, as in sports, is another connection Saint Paul makes when, in looking back over his life, he says, "I have finished the marathon."[7] Our faith journey is no sprint, he suggests here; instead, it's an endurance run. Running, in fact, seems to have been a favorite sport of Saint Paul. We don't know if he was a participant or only a fan, but either way, he refers to running often. For instance, when discussing the need to be fully committed and not half-hearted about faith matters, he insisted: "Run so as to win" (1 Cor 9:24). He cautioned some of his readers that, although they had been "running well" (Gal 5:7), they now seemed to be backsliding in their faith lives. And when stressing that our lives have purpose when lived according to God's plan, Saint Paul concluded: "I did not run in vain or labor in vain" (Phil 2:16).

As Saint Paul makes clear, sports can most certainly teach us lessons we can apply to our faith journey, such as the benefits of pushing through difficulties, training for a goal, keeping one's eyes on the prize, playing by the rules, exhibiting good sportsmanship, and being gracious in both victory and defeat, because winning isn't everything. As words attributed to Mother Teresa remind us, "God doesn't call us to be successful. He calls us to be faithful."

Playing sports and simply exercising and making healthy life choices can help strengthen our faith. This is due to the connection between our bodies and our minds. How we feel physically can affect how we feel mentally, which can impact our relationship with God. For instance, Saint Teresa of Avila noted that a bad headache can handicap our praying. On the flip side, there have been times when I have been praying the rosary while running and felt deeply loved by God. Sure, it may have been a "runner's high," but then God can speak to us through our feelings. He gave them to us, after all.

When it comes to praying while running, I am not alone. One person ran from coast to coast in 121 days, and he prayed the entire way![8] There are other ways to connect faith and sports as well. One friend of mine listens to religious podcasts while biking to work. And groups of priests have formed exhibition basketball and baseball teams to encourage young people in their faith and encourage them to consider becoming a priest or a sister.

Whether we're in training every day or simply enjoy watching others play their games, we can allow sports to impact our faith. After all, in the words of Blessed John Paul II, "Every Christian is called to be a strong athlete of Christ."[9]

 CHAPTER 34

# Take a Hike

With whistles, clicks, and hoots, he could mimic the distinctive call of every bird in North America. Or so it seemed to us, the students in his high school biology classes. Our teacher would take us on nature trips in his aging, bright-orange VW wagon, offering us edible roots and bugs, which we typically declined. And through it all, he lived and shared his deep Christian faith. It permeated everything he did, and we kids knew it.

He'd sometimes tell his compelling conversion story, which is fitting for one who so deeply loves nature. When he was a teenager, he was unsure about God, until one day when he was deep in thought and walking along a beach. As he took in the beauty around him and considered nature's order and complexity, it became crystal clear to him that there not only had to be a God, but that this God must surely be good. Filled with joy, he leaped and shouted across the sand.

Just like my biology teacher, we can be convinced of God's existence through God's creation. "Ever since the creation of the world," argued Saint Paul, "(God's) invisible attributes of eternal power and divinity have been able to be understood and perceived in what he has made" (Rm 1:20). Yet God's creation can also speak to us of God's majesty, beauty, and awesomeness. And God's creation, which he declared to be "good," can reveal that God himself is good.

This was the conclusion of the author of Psalm 8, in the Bible's Old Testament. As he gazed up at a nighttime sky, he was overwhelmed by the realization that he mattered to a God responsible for something so immense: "When I see . . . the moon and stars that you set in place—What is man that you are mindful of him?"(Ps 8: 4–5). When that was written, it was assumed that the stars traveled across a huge dome in the sky. But consider what we know today. Astronomers conclude that, throughout the entire universe, there are at least sixteen billion galaxies with perhaps one hundred billion stars apiece. These galaxies inhabit a space which is over nine billion light years from one edge to the other. And since light travels at a speed of over six million miles per year, the universe is so amazingly huge that I can't even begin to comprehend its magnitude.

We can worry that the Creator of such a cosmos would write us off as worthless or too insignificant to bother with. Perhaps that's one reason why God came to live among us as he did. He didn't appear like we might expect a God who established such a huge universe to appear—with thunder and lightning or some amazing display of power. Instead, God became small, like we are, by entering our world as a tiny baby. He loves us because we're important to him, because we're precious in his sight, because he has a plan for each one of our lives. We might say that, thanks to Jesus, we know that the God responsible for such an immense creation is filled with an immensity of love.

Reflecting on creation can lead us to give thanks and praise to God. It can happen by gazing through a telescope or peering into a microscope. We might find ourselves moved and inspired by the colors of a rainbow, the stillness of a forest, the majesty of a mountain, or the vast expanse of the sea. The sunrise has spoken to generations of the resurrection of Jesus, who himself thought that the lilies of the field were more beautiful than King Solomon in all his royal splendor. As Scripture exclaims, creation itself glorifies God just by being what God created it to be: "Let the rivers clap their hands" and "the mountains shout with them for joy" (Ps 98:8).

Creation is God's gift to us. He intends for us to enjoy it, benefit from it, and share its resources fairly with everyone. We're therefore invited to care for it in a way that respects the needs of all people, including those of future generations. "Preservation of the environment, promotion of sustainable development, and particular attention to climate change," explains Pope Benedict XVI, "are matters of grave concern for the entire human family."[1] If we make the effort to care for God's creation, we'll appreciate that it is a blessing to be treasured, not a resource to be exploited. Creation will remind us of God's loving care for us, and we will be filled with gratitude and grow in faith.

Saint Francis of Assisi, like many others, knew this well. Tradition tells of Saint Francis preaching to the birds of the field and thanking God for "Brother Sun" and "Sister Moon." Saint John of the Cross would take his fellow monks on outdoor hikes into Spain's Andalucian hills to contemplate God in the night sky. Jesus himself would often seek mountaintops on which to pray, and on the night he was betrayed and arrested, he chose to pray in a garden.

We, too, on occasion, might seek out a garden or a mountaintop on which to pray. While there we might find, as John Denver famously sang, that as we talk to God we'll hear his "casual reply."[2] Indeed, we can hear God's whispers through just about any element of his creation. After all, it is his handiwork, and his fingerprints are all over it.

So take a hike! Smell the roses. Listen to the wind in the trees. Visit a zoo or a planetarium. Lie in the grass and absorb the sights, sounds, and smells around you. Sit in the sand and gaze at the ocean. Even tune into a nature show on television. And while we're at it, we can reduce, reuse, and recycle, flip off the lights when we leave the room, and shut off the water when we brush our teeth. All this can nourish our faith and lead us to exclaim: "Our LORD, how awesome in your name through all the earth!" (Ps 8:2).

## CHAPTER 35

# Visit a Museum

Although he had been raised a Christian, his faith hadn't transitioned with him to college. He found himself immersed in campus life, and Christian values didn't have much impact on what he did. That changed one day, however, when he visited a local art museum and encountered a painting of Mary, the Mother of Jesus. He found himself mesmerized by both the beauty of the art and the woman it portrayed. He was moved to tears, and from that day on his life's journey began to take a different direction. That encounter with beauty, expressed through art, renewed the faith of his childhood, and ultimately led him into the Catholic Church.[1]

As this young man learned, beautiful art can speak to us of God. God created beauty, and an encounter with anything beautiful can become an encounter with God himself. Beautiful art can call forth from us wonder and awe and draw us toward the God who is truly wonderful and awesome. To borrow an image from the ancient philosopher Plato, art can give wings to the soul. That's why Catholic churches are designed to be beautiful. Through the ages, different cultures have expressed beauty in their houses of worship in different ways, but the intention has always been the same.

Art within our churches is certainly decorative and can help make a worship environment appealing and attractive. But it serves other purposes too. For instance, art is one way the truths and stories of our faith are proclaimed. In earlier centuries, when most people were unable to read, they would learn the history of salvation and the lives of Jesus, the saints, and the great figures of the Bible from the carvings, statues, paintings, tapestries, and stained glass windows they encountered where they worshiped.

We can still learn in this same way today—especially those of us whom educators would describe as "visual learners." It's often said that "a picture is worth a thousand words," and the signs, symbols, and images found in a church can powerfully teach and remind us of all that God has revealed about himself and his plan for our salvation. Dana Gioia, a Catholic poet and former chairperson of the National Endowment of the Arts, even claims that "Michelangelo and El Greco . . . (and) the anonymous architects of Chartres and Notre Dame, have awakened more souls to the divine than all the papal encyclicals."[2]

Yet, while art in churches can both teach and decorate, perhaps its most important function is to lift our hearts and minds to God, enable us to "worship the LORD in the beauty of holiness,"[3] and lead us into contemplation and prayer.

Some, however, have concluded that art in churches is unnecessary and even wrong. Consider a great church in the heart of Geneva, Switzerland. It had once been a colorfully decorated Catholic cathedral. But then, centuries ago, it passed into the hands of Christians who objected to the ornamentation. They insisted that it would distract the worshipers from focusing on the word of God as proclaimed in the Bible and explained in the sermon. They even feared it might lead to idol worship! So the church was completely stripped, leaving only cold stone and colorless windows.

Years ago, I had an opportunity to tour this church. I had looked forward to my visit, but on arriving I left as quickly as I could because I found the environment sad and depressing. As I made my way out, however, I passed through an adjoining chapel that had been built by a later generation, and it was far from drab. I recall the ceiling in particular; it was painted in different patterns and colors, and seeing it lifted my spirits. I felt as one does on a bright, warm, spring day after a long, hard, and dreary winter.

The Catholic Church embraces color. The different days and seasons of the Church year, for instance, are distinguished by colors: red and green, white and violet, and sometimes even rose and gold. We embrace these visual "markers" because we can appreciate that God can touch our lives through our senses of sight, smell, taste, and touch. Consider the sacraments, through which God fills us with grace through bread and wine, oil and water, gestures and words. Art doesn't fill us with grace, of course, but it can move our spirits. That's why Pope John Paul II described art as a "pre-sacrament," and our churches are adorned, at a bare minimum, with a crucifix, a depiction of Mary, and the Stations of the Cross.[4]

Religious art, whether we encounter it inside or outside of a church, can proclaim that the world God created is both good and beautiful. It can serve as an antidote to the saturation of mundane images we're bombarded with daily, which can be commercial, crass, and exploitative. And it can lift our faith when it sags. According to Pope Benedict XVI, visiting churches, art galleries, and museums can be "moments of grace, incentives to strengthen our bond and our dialogue with the Lord."[5]

Since that's true, consider a trip to an art museum to appreciate and contemplate what's on exhibit—whether it's explicitly religious or not. Make a little pilgrimage to a church known for its beauty, and take a renewed look at the art in your own church. Examine the Stations of the Cross you may have passed by so many times; stay after Mass a minute and admire the statues and pictures; if there's stained glass, gaze and consider what it depicts. You may be surprised at what you'll see and what you may learn. Consider decorating your home with religious images too. It will remind you of God's love and that we're a part of a worldwide family of faith. And it may inspire your guests as well.

"Beauty is fleeting," we lament, and sometimes it is, this side of heaven. But any beauty can also point us to that which never fades—our God, whom Saint Augustine described as "Beauty ever ancient, ever new."[6]

 CHAPTER 36

# Bon Appétit

As he knew that the Lord would soon call him home, Saint Francis of Assisi began to get his affairs in order. He sent a letter to a dear friend in Rome, Lady Jacoba de Settesoli, inviting her to visit him before he died. He asked her to bring some practical items, such as a sackcloth shroud for him to be buried in and wax candles for his funeral Mass. His final request, however, was for a special treat: almond marzipan sweets, of which Saint Francis was especially fond.

That a saint celebrated for his extreme simplicity of life and his embrace of poverty for the sake of God's kingdom would request candy for his final hours is not just an endearing biographical footnote, but also a sign of the positive role food can play in our lives, including our spiritual lives.

Food and shared meals certainly featured significantly in our Lord's life and ministry. A great deal of his teaching, as Luke's Gospel presents it, was given in the context of meals at the homes of others. Jesus enjoyed these meals so much that his detractors challenged him about it. "Look," they mocked, "he is a glutton and a drunkard" (Lk 7:34).

Jesus was also criticized not just for enjoying meals but for eating them with certain people—"tax collectors and sinners" (Mt 11:19), to use the words of his critics. In his day, to share a dinner at table was an expression of fellowship and belonging. To eat with another was a sign that one welcomed and embraced the person as a friend. That Jesus ate with cultural outcasts and those on the margins of society was an expression of his love for everyone—and a real source of scandal.

It was at a traditional Jewish Passover meal with his friends that Jesus gave us the gift of Holy Eucharist, and through the ages Christians have celebrated their love for Jesus, and those of his saints, with festive meals and special foods. Think of the lamb dishes and eggs associated with Easter, or the traditional breads of Poland and Ukraine for that day. Mexican and Guatemalan Catholics celebrate *Los Posadas* ("The Inns") with tamales, stews, and piñatas filled with fruit, nuts, and candy in recollection of Mary and Joseph's search for a place to stay in Bethlehem. On Christmas Eve, Italians celebrate the Feast of the Seven Fishes, and on Christmas Day, the English enjoy mincemeat pies and Germans serve *stollen*, both prepared in an oblong shape to recall the manger that served as Jesus' crib. Foods have been used to teach the faith too. It's said that the pretzel's twists were first made by a monk of the Middle Ages to encourage children to fold their arms in prayer, while the treat's three holes taught them of the three Persons of the Trinity. And the curved ends of candy canes are shaped like a shepherd's crook to remind boys and girls that Christmas is a celebration of the birth of Jesus, the Good Shepherd.

Our Lord taught us to pray for our "daily bread," and the food our heavenly Father gives is a sign of his love and care for us. It's certainly essential for health and life; but for human beings, food is far more than just fuel. Food and meals can unite us as families and communities and are at the heart of any celebration. It's for good reason that Jesus described heaven as a festive wedding banquet, while in his parable of the Prodigal Son, the wayward son's return home is honored by a feast upon the "fattened calf" (see Lk 15:11–32).

Food obviously nourishes our bodies, but it can nourish souls as well. One way we can allow food to do this is by rediscovering the value of the shared meal. For Jesus and his companions, meals were leisurely events that solidified the bonds of family and friendship. Our contemporary experience, however, is quite different. Busy schedules often dictate that we eat on the run, frequently alone, and sometimes on the dashboard as we prepare to race off to the next event or commitment. Or, when we do eat together, we're tempted to park ourselves in front of the TV instead of speaking with each other.

Eating together, however, allows us to communicate and connect in ways we can't by phone or email. When families make dining together a priority, studies indicate that the children enjoy a stronger sense of security and belonging, are more likely to stay out of trouble, and even get better grades. And families can certainly use mealtime to share faith—beginning by praying grace.

If done in the right spirit, cooking for others is a way to show our love for them and express welcome and hospitality, in imitation of our gracious God, who loves, welcomes, and cares for us. It's often said that the way to a man's heart is through his stomach, but good food, lovingly served, can touch anyone's heart. By celebrating the traditional meals our culture or heritage associates with its Catholic heritage, we can cultivate our faith—and pass it on to the next generation. And through preparing meals, by taking our time and working with raw ingredients, we can come to appreciate that food is truly God's gift to us.

Since food is God's gift to us, we treasure it and honor the giver by enjoying it in moderation. To feast is fine! But if we feast every day, we may come to treat food with indifference or allow it to become a compulsion. And daily feasting may blind us to the needs of those who have less access to food than we do and who go to bed hungry. As Saint Teresa of Avila is said to have quipped, while there is a time for partridge (a delicacy of her day), there is also a time for porridge.[1]

Yet whether we find ourselves dining on partridge or porridge on any given day, our food can feed our faith, and allow us to "taste and see that the LORD is good" (Ps 34:8 *RSV*).

 CHAPTER 37

# Laugh Out Loud

**M**y kids were once playing with an electric keyboard in our house, and it sounded to me like they were playing "spooky music." "We must be in a haunted house!" I said. "Oh Daddy," came the reply, "it's not a haunted house. It's church!"

As a priest, that isn't exactly what I wanted to hear. But my children's words reminded me that some people think of Christianity as a somber, glum affair. And for some people, it *is* a somber, glum affair. Saint Teresa of Avila, a joyful person, found herself surrounded by such people in her work and in her convent. She is said to have prayed, "From sour-faced saints, good Lord, deliver us!"

The truth is, God made us to be happy. God himself is happy, and he wants us to share in his happiness. Yet we can forget this at times, especially since our faith places a positive value on suffering and calls us to sacrifice and repent of our sins. We can lose sight of the fact that the core message of the Gospel is not suffering and death but resurrection and new life. Our faith is, of course, serious business. But it shouldn't make us sad.

Years ago, the Catholic humorist Erma Bombeck wrote of a little boy she saw at a Mass who kept turning around and smiling at everyone. He was being well-behaved; he was just enjoying smiling at people. But then, all of a sudden, his mother yanked him around and hissed, "Stop that grinning. You're in church!"[1] It's because of attitudes like this that some insist that laughing with sinners is preferable to crying with saints.

But real saints are happy people. Think about it: if Christians were all sad sacks, the Church would have expired long ago. And if signs were put up in front of churches that read: "Come and Be Unhappy With Us," we'd wind up with a lot of empty pews pretty fast—and I'd be out of a job. And, if you're wondering, it is okay to smile in church, as I had to remind a congregation one Easter Sunday. At the beginning of Mass, I processed down the main aisle and sprinkled people with holy water. As I did, I was struck by how many long, gloomy, and sad faces I saw. So after I was done, I announced: "I just want to remind you that Jesus is risen. It's okay to smile!"

Celebrating Jesus' resurrection is always reason to smile. Think back to the first Easter Sunday, when two unnamed disciples were approached by Jesus as they were walking to the town of Emmaus (see Lk 24:13–35). They didn't believe that Jesus had risen, and they certainly didn't see that it was Jesus himself walking alongside them. So when Jesus asked them what they were talking about, we're told that "they stood still, looking sad" (Lk 24:17, *RSV*). Just like so many of the people I saw at that one Easter morning Mass.

But that's not the end of the story. After the travelers arrived in Emmaus, the two disciples recognized Jesus in "the breaking of the bread"—the Eucharist—and were so filled with joy that they ran to tell their friends. The risen Jesus had replaced their sadness with joy! And the same can be true for us. As Blessed Teresa of Calcutta counsels, "Never let anything so fill you with pain or sorrow so as to make you forget the joy of the Risen Christ."[2]

In Catholic teaching, joy is one of the "fruits" of the Holy Spirit; it's a sure sign of God's active presence in one's life. Joy, in fact, is one reason why so many people were attracted to him in the first place. Joy brings people together; we're drawn to those we find joyful and happy. Misery may indeed love company, but most company prefers joy.

One way we can cultivate joy, and express it in our lives, is through humor and laughter. Humor certainly brings with it what we might call "natural" benefits, such as better health, longer life, and the companionship of friends. But humor and laughter can have a positive impact on our faith life as well, because good humor, like good faith, requires a good dose of humility. Humor can lead us not to take ourselves too seriously, which in turn can make us more humble. In fact, "humor" and "humility" share a common Latin root: *humus*, which means "soil" or "earth." That's only fitting because humble people, like truly humorous people, are "down to earth."

Saint Thomas Aquinas, one of Catholicism's great historical thinkers, even suggested that a lack of humor might be, at times, somewhat sinful. Such people, he observed, become "burdensome to others, by offering no pleasure to others, and by hindering their enjoyment . . . they are boorish and rude."[3] That doesn't mean that we all need to be stand-up comics! Pope

Benedict XVI admits that he's not one to crack a lot of jokes. But at the same time, he appreciates the need "to see the funny side of life and its joyful dimension and not to take everything too tragically."[4]

To be sure, there have been plenty of Catholics able to deliver a good punch line. Saint Philip Neri was one; he died with a Bible and a joke book by his bedside. In his work with troubled youth, Saint John Bosco used both humor and magic. "Laugh and grow strong!" was the advice given to novices by the founder of the Jesuits, Saint Ignatius Loyola.[5] And when he was asked how many people worked at the Vatican, Blessed Pope John XXIII famously replied, "About half!"[6]

To enjoy humor doesn't mean that Catholics don't get unhappy. We do, of course. Catholics get depressed; Catholics get sad. Catholics weep, just as Jesus wept at the tomb of his friend, Lazarus (see Jn 11:17–35). Yet even in our darkest moments, the root of our joy remains, so long as our faith remains: faith that an eternity of joy has been promised us; faith that can be fed, every time we laugh out loud.

 CHAPTER 38

# Throw a Party

The suggestion to my parish committee was to have the youth group make pancakes for the community on "Shrove Tuesday," the old English title for the day before Ash Wednesday. One committee member, however, had a better plan: scrap the pancake supper, and replace it with a Mardi Gras (Fat Tuesday) party. Which we did—with masks and costumes, beads and doubloons, a king cake, crawfish by the boxful, beer by the pitcher, and a roast suckling pig. A great time was had by all, the parish family bonded, and there was much music and laughter. And everyone made it to Mass the next day!

Celebration is at the heart of Catholic living, and Jesus himself set the tone. He performed his first miracle at a wedding festival. He described heaven itself as a wedding banquet, and he spoke of heaven's rejoicing whenever one sinner repents. Jesus concluded a parable with a woman throwing a spontaneous neighborhood party after finding a treasured lost coin (see Lk 15:8–9). In his story of the Prodigal Son, the over-joyed father hosts a feast upon his wayward son's return home.

Following this lead, Catholics have distinguished them-selves as a people who love a good celebration. Catholic cultures of every nation have given rise to traditional festivals to cele-brate special days in the Church's calendar, many of which are called, quite appropriately, "feasts." And there's nothing dull about them! They're filled with sights and sounds, parades and processions, dancing and dining. As the quintessentially English G. K. Chesterton came to understand, in Catholicism a pint, a pipe, and the cross can all fit together. [1]

A traditional "call and response" enjoyed by black Christians begins with the leader proclaiming, "God is good!" To which the assembly responds: "All the time!" God is indeed good, and celebrations are a way we can celebrate God's goodness. After all, God's goodness should call forth from us both gratitude and joy. A Christian, according to Saint Augustine, should be an alleluia from head to foot.[2]

If we can't find it within ourselves to celebrate, and if joy is absent from our life, our spiritual health might be a bit off. Author Ronald Rolheiser tells of a young nun for whom this was the case.[3] She was a sister in a religious order that was deeply committed to serving the poor. Her community inten-tionally lived in poverty, and she herself ministered to political prisoners in Asia.

Rolheiser met her at a conference in Belgium. For four days the conference attendees worked hard, but the fifth day was devoted to sightseeing and was concluded by a banquet at a fine restaurant. The nun, however, refused to participate. She stayed on the tour bus, angry that those whom she had thought were committed to social justice would be so extravagant and, to her mind, wasteful. But as she sat and stewed, the thought came to her that if Jesus were there, he'd be inside with the group, enjoying their company and the meal. She realized then that something was frozen inside her, and she vowed to change.

God did not wish for her, nor does he wish for us, to be among the "frozen chosen." Commitment to the poor doesn't preclude a spirit of celebration. Think of Saint Francis of Assisi. No one was more committed to loving the poor than he was. At the same time, he was literally brimming over with joy and would at times burst into dance and song. And consider an episode from the life of Jesus, when his friend Mary poured costly oil on his feet in a gesture of love. Judas Iscariot protested that the oil could have been sold and the money given to the poor. But Jesus would have none of that. "Leave her alone," he insisted. "You always have the poor with you" (Jn 12:7–8).

Jesus wasn't saying that we shouldn't care about the poor. He was simply endorsing Mary's right to celebrate their friendship. After all, Jesus elsewhere taught that we should make a point to invite the poor whenever we throw a dinner party (see Lk 14:12–14). Here he suggests that a proper spirit of celebration will actually lead us to care more, not less, about the needs of others. Celebrating God's goodness will make us more grateful for his gifts. And gratitude breeds generosity.

Celebration is good for the soul. Just as "all work and no play make Jack a dull boy," a faith life without celebration can grow stale and lifeless, focused more on doing one's duty than responding to grace and love. Duty is important, to be sure! But it cannot stand alone. Saint Paul knew that, which is why he could insist: "Rejoice in the Lord always. I shall say it again: rejoice!" (Phil 4:4).

The father of a bride once approached me the Sunday after I had presided at his daughter's wedding. The celebration itself had been beautiful, from start to finish. The bride and groom were beaming, the sun was shining, the liturgy was filled with joy, everyone was happy, and the reception was loads of fun. It was, quite literally, one of the best days of that man's life. He asked me: "Why can't every day be like that?"

Why? Because while heaven will be like an eternal wedding party, this side of heaven is more like life after a wedding: there's better, and there's worse; there's richer, and there's poorer; there's sickness, and there's health. Heavenly days, however, remind us of what we long for in faith, and our earthly celebrations can give us a small taste of the good things yet to come.

So by all means, celebrate! Create a little bit of heaven here on earth. Commemorate birthdays and anniversaries, baptisms and graduations, farewells and new beginnings. Invite the neighbors over, organize a block party, plan a parish picnic, decorate for the changing seasons. Enjoy a family fun night, dance in the living room, make popcorn. It's all good! And it's certainly very Catholic. As Hilaire Belloc wrote:

> Wherever the Catholic sun doth shine,
> There's always laughter and good red wine.
> At least I've always found it so.
> *Benedicamus Domino!*

## CHAPTER 39

# Sing a Song

What do you like best about Christmas? The lights and decorations? Getting together with family and friends? Buying gifts for loved ones? All the traditional foods and treats? Midnight Mass? For many people, Christmas music is what they love most—as heard over the airwaves and sung by children, choirs, and carolers at the door.

After all, the birth of Jesus is the "reason for the season," and that's certainly worth singing about! On Christmas, we celebrate that "light" and "life" were brought to us by the "Word" who "became flesh," "made his dwelling among us," and revealed the "glory as of the Father's only Son" (Jn 1:14).

The words quoted above are taken, by the way, from the first chapter of John's Gospel, which most likely incorporated an ancient Christian hymn that the Gospel's first readers would have been familiar with. And if that's the case, then Christians were singing about Christmas before the New Testament was even finished!

Then again, there was singing on the first Christmas itself. Scripture shares how angels in heaven sang "Glory to God in the highest" (Lk 2:14), a refrain that begins one of the traditional prayers for Mass. And, after the shepherds found the infant Jesus lying in a manger, they were "glorifying and praising God" (Lk 2:20), which surely included their bursting into song. Mary herself burst into song before Jesus was even born. "My soul proclaims the greatness of the Lord," she exclaimed to her cousin Elizabeth, "my spirit rejoices in God my savior" (Lk 1:46b–47).

What we celebrate at Christmas is so wonderful that we seem almost compelled to sing about it. This should come as no surprise, as we seek to express through music so many things in our faith tradition and human experience. When we're in love, we sing love songs. When we're sad, we sing the blues. "It feels good to sing about something that hurts so bad," admits '50s rocker-turned-Catholic-author Dion. The blues, he adds, are "the naked cry of the human heart longing to be united to God."[1]

Of course, if they are a "longing to be united to God," then the blues will be sung only this side of heaven. There will be plenty of other things to sing about in heaven, and all of them will be joyful. We're given glimpses of heaven in Scripture, one of which features a host of angels and saints worshiping God with a song that begins "Holy, Holy, Holy"—a song echoed at each and every Mass.

Mass, as a matter of fact, is where heaven and earth meet. Around the altar, we join our voices with the heavenly host in their eternal praise of God. "Singing itself is almost like flying, rising up to God," explained Pope Benedict XVI. "It is in some way an anticipation of eternity when we will be able to 'unceasingly sing God's praise.'"[2] Those words were spoken by a true music lover who is an accomplished pianist, adores Mozart, and recalls with fondness his father's playing the zither for his family when he was a child.

Pope Benedict XVI's words about "flying" and "rising up to God" resonate with me in light of an experience I had in seminary at a performance of Rachmaninov's "Vespers," sung by a Russian choir. Never having heard the piece before, I didn't know what to expect. Yet during the magnificent performance I felt as if I had somehow been lifted up out of my body. Others had a similar experience, I believe, because when the singing stopped, no one clapped. Instead, there was complete silence for what seemed like a full minute. That silence was eventually followed by thunderous applause. But first, we had to descend back to earth from heaven.

As I learned that evening, music can transport us outside ourselves by evoking wonder and awe. It can give rise to powerful feelings and allow powerful feelings to be expressed. Active singing has been shown to reduce stress and improve moods. In other words, we can lift our spirits by lifting our voices! And those who sing in choirs have a higher level of satisfaction with their lives than the general public.

Music and singing can impact and benefit faith as well. Good songs can be an effective method to teach and learn the faith because they can proclaim truths in a memorable way, since melody and poetry make things easier to remember. For instance, when I took chemistry in high school, I had to memorize the periodic table of elements. Yet I can't recall a thing about it now! However, I can recall the lyrics of lots of songs I listened to as a kid on my AM transistor radio. Better yet, I can remember hymns that I was first introduced to in childhood. It's for this reason that some of the Church's greatest teachers, such as Saints Ambrose, Augustine, and Thomas Aquinas, were also writers of hymns.

In addition to teaching the faith, music and singing can also strengthen faith when it feels fragile. Sister Thea Bowman learned this when she turned to her African-American culture's traditional Gospel spirituals for help during her struggle with cancer. "When I hurt, I like to sing some of the old songs," she confessed. "I find that prayer and song can take me beyond the pain."[3] As she experienced, music can be a window through which we encounter God's healing and love when we need it most. This is especially true at Mass: "This common, sung expression of faith within (worship) strengthens our faith when it grows weak,"[4] explain the U.S. bishops.

Singing the same song can bind a community more closely together when it worships together. A congregation forms one body when they sing with one voice, praising our one God. Indeed, singing expresses praise like nothing else can. Jesus himself sang, and he invites us to sing too—even if we think we can't sing at all. Maybe that's why Saint Augustine is said to have exclaimed: "He who sings, prays twice!"[5]

# Different Strokes
# for Different Folks

Human beings are like snowflakes—no two of us are exactly alike. We may have similarities, of course, but at our core, we are unique and irreplaceable. The DNA upon which we are constructed is different from the DNA of any other person who has lived before, is living today, or who will ever live in the future. That's even true for identical twins! God planned it that way because God loves variety. And because God made us just the way we are, God loves us just for being us. "God loves each one of us," promised Saint Augustine, "as if there were only one of us to love."[1]

God created each of us in his own image. But even though we are reflections of the eternal God who never changes, that doesn't mean that we've all come from the same mold or are cookie-cutter copies of each other. Although created in the image of the one God, we ourselves are one-of-a-kind. This means that each of us presents to the world something about God that no one else can. In a sense, we might say that if any one of us had never been born, God's reflection in the world would somehow be incomplete.

But the truth is, we have been born, and our being here is no accident. We are here because God wants us to be here. In his goodness and love, we have been "wonderfully made," as Psalm139:14 beautifully puts it. We aren't disposable, insignificant or dime-a-dozen, and our lives are meant to have a purpose.

At the heart of our life's purpose is learning to love and serve God and one another, as expressed through a rich and vibrant faith. That's why God is always reaching out to us, in any number of ways, to bring us to faith and fill us with his gift. And because we're unique, the ways that God will seek to touch our lives will honor, and reflect, our individuality. That's why Pope Benedict XVI could write that each believer is "always traveling his own personal itinerary of faith."[2]

Consider the first disciples whom Jesus invited to follow him. As it was, they were two sets of brothers: Simon and Andrew, and James and John. They were fishermen, and when Jesus spoke to them while they were tending their nets, Mark's Gospel described them as literally dropping everything and following Jesus on the spot. But why? Scripture doesn't tell us. All we can do is guess.

It could be that they were compelled by Jesus's call to repentance. Perhaps they were convinced in their hearts that they needed to turn their lives around and start living in a more righteous manner, and the preaching of Jesus was a real catalyst for change. Or maybe they were inspired by his proclamation that the kingdom of God had broken into the world. The kingdom's promise of justice, liberation, and peace would have certainly appealed to first-century fishermen in Galilee, who typically worked under oppressively difficult conditions and were chronically underpaid and overtaxed.

This side of heaven, we'll never know exactly what inspired Simon, Andrew, James, and John to become disciples of the Lord that day. It wouldn't be surprising if each of them had a different reason, because that's true of us. Every person who comes to faith does so for different reasons, because every person is different. We have different histories, different life circumstances, different gifts, different weaknesses, and different personalities.

At the end of the day, the faith all Catholics profess is one and the same; there is but "one Lord, one faith, one baptism" (Eph 4:5). But the one Lord is happy to lead us to the one faith by any number of means. There are many different paths leading up the same mountain. As G. K. Chesterton observed, "The Church is a house with a hundred gates, and no two men enter at exactly the same angle."[3]

Saint Thomas Aquinas taught that, using our reason, there are five ways we can know that God exists. Yet there are an endless number of ways that we can come to faith in God and be embraced by his love. That has been a main point of this book: to highlight some of the avenues through which we can awaken ourselves to God's presence all around us and open ourselves more and more to the gift of faith. Certain of these avenues may have already been known to you and others may be new. Some will appeal to us more than others, because we're unique. That's to be expected, and that's okay. Because when it comes to coming to faith, there's no "one size fits all."

People can even come to faith through means of which the Church may not necessarily approve, as Flannery O'Connor observed.[4] Take Venerable Francis Libermann, for instance, who is advancing toward official sainthood. Libermann was raised Jewish, and he took his first step toward Catholicism by reading Jean-Jacques Rousseau's *Emile*, a work frowned upon by Catholics in his day.[5] An even more extreme example is that of Peter Hitchens, brother of outspoken atheist Christopher Hitchens, who wrote *God Is Not Great*. In his own book, *The Rage Against God: How Atheism Led Me to Faith*, Peter explains how his former atheism, and that of his brother, led him back to the Christian faith of his youth.[6]

God can certainly write straight with crooked lines, as the old saying goes. Thankfully, God can work with the crooked lines we sometimes present to him, because he knows us better than we know ourselves. He made us the way we are, everything he makes is good, and when all is said and done, all God wants is for us to be the person he created us to be: a saint, but one unlike any other. "Perfection," concluded Saint Therese of Lisieux, "consists . . . in being what [God] wills us to be."[7]

God says to us: "Be yourself!" And if we do that, living as God wishes us to live, we'll find ourselves living with *confidence*, in every sense of its Latin roots: *con* (with), and *fide* (faith)—with faith.

# Notes

### Chapter 1: Take the Offer

1. Gretchen R. Crowe, "Admit Faith Is Weak, New York Archbishop Tells Young People in Madrid," Catholic News Service story, August 17, 2011.

2. Brian Kolodiejchuk, M.C., ed., *Mother Teresa: Come Be My Light* (New York: Doubleday, 2007), 193.

### Chapter 3: Tend Your Garden

1. Jeff Kurowski, "Jubilee Invites Spiritual Renewal," *The Compass: Official Newspaper of the Catholic Diocese of Green Bay*, February 25, 2000.

### Chapter 4: Take Baby Steps

1. Julian of Norwich, *Revelations of Divine Love*, Grace Warrack trans. (First published in 1901), 33. Accessed at http://www.ccel.org/ccel/julian/revelations.

### Chapter 5: Don't Get Off the Bus

1. Friedrich Nietzsche, *Thus Spake Zarathustra*, trans. by Thomas Common (New York: The Modern Library, 1917), 98.

2. See Gordon W. Allport, *The Individual and His Religion* (New York: The Macmillan Company, 1960), 73.

3. Quoted in Harold Victor Martin, *Kierkegaard, the Melancholy Dane* (University of Michigan: Philosophical Library, 1950), 86.

4. Leslie Houlden, ed., *Austin Farrer: The Essential Sermons* (London: SPCK, 1991), 171.

## Chapter 6: Make the Choice

1. See B. J. Thomas, *Hooked on a Feeling*, Scepter Records SCE 12230 A, 1968, 45 rpm.

2. See The Righteous Brothers, *You've Lost that Lovin' Feelin'*, Philles Records (A Division of Phil Specter Productions), 1964, 45 rpm.

## Chapter 7: Follow Like Sheep

1. See "The God Debate," *Newsweek*, April 9, 2007, 63. Accessed at http://www.thedailybeast.com/newsweek/2007/04/08/the-god-debate.html.

## Chapter 8: Don't Look Down!

1. Pope Benedict XVI, *Saved In Hope, Spe Salvi* (Boston: Pauline Books & Media, 2007), no. 39.

## Chapter 9: Change Your Prescription

1. Thomas à Kempis, *Imitation of Christ*, Book II, ch. 7.

2. John E. Rotelle, O.S.A, ed., L. Edmund Hill, O.P., trans., *The Works of Saint Augustine: A Translation for the 21st Century*, Sermons 111/7 (230–272B) on Liturgical Seasons (Hyde Park, NY: New City Press, 1993), 41.

3. Kieran Kavanaugh, O.C.D., and Otilio Rodriguez, O.C.D., trans., *The Collected Works of Saint Teresa of Avila* (Washington, DC: Institute of Carmelite Studies, 1985), vol. 3:119–120.

4. See Jean-Francois Six, ed., *The Spiritual Autobiography of Charles de Foucauld* (Frederick, MD: Word Among Us Press, 2004), 70.

## Chapter 10: Eat Some Pie

1. Blessed Mother Teresa, Sean-Patrick Lovett, ed., *The Best Gift Is Love: Meditations by Mother Teresa* (Ann Arbor, MI: Servant Publications, 1993), 56.

## Chapter 13: Sweep Up the Crumbs

1. Saint Francis de Sales, *The Consoling Thoughts of St. Francis de Sales (Book 3)*, ed. Jean-Joseph Huguet (Dublin: M. H. Gill & Son, 1877), 233.

2. Robert J. Wicks, *Touching the Holy* (Notre Dame, IN: Sorin Books, 1992), 60–61.

## Chapter 14: Get Soaked in Scripture

1. Anna B. Warner and David Rutherford McGuire, *Jesus Loves Me,* with music by William B. Bradbury, 1862.

2. *Catechism of the Catholic Church,* (Boston: Pauline Books & Media, 1994), no. 104.

3. See *Dei Verbum* 25; Phil 3:8; *Catechism of the Catholic Church* no. 112; and Saint Jerome, *Commentariorum in Isaiam* libri xviii prol.:PL 24,17B.

## Chapter 15: Take Bread for the Journey

1. See Oscar Lukefahr, C.M., *We Worship: A Guide to the Catholic Mass* (Liguori, MO: Liguori Publications, 2004), 94.

2. Pope John Paul II, "Holy Mass at The Living History Farms," in Des Moines, Iowa. October 25, 1979, no. 3. Accessed at http://www.vatican.va/holy_father/john_paul_ii/homilies/1979/documents/hf_jp-ii_hom_19791004_usa-des-moines_en.html on January 2013.

3. Saint Augustine of Hippo, *The Confessions of St. Augustine*, Book I, ch. 1.

4. *Catechism of the Catholic Church*, no. 1323.

## Chapter 16: Read a Book

1. See Michael Morris, O.P., "The Carpenter's Shop," *Magnificat*, issue unknown.

2. Saint Augustine, *Sermo* 43, 7, 9: PL 38, 257–258; see also *Catechism of the Catholic Church*, no. 158.

3. See G. K. Chesterton, *Orthodoxy* (London: Bodley Head, 1908), 16.

## Chapter 17: Don't Read a Book

1. Lawrence Cunningham, *Things Seen and Unseen: A Catholic Theologian's Notebook* (Notre Dame, IN: Sorin Books, 2010), 38.

2. *Imitation of Christ,* Book I, ch. 3.

## Chapter 18: Look Over Your Shoulder

1. Pope Benedict XVI, "Wednesday Angelus Address," October 12, 2011, on Psalm 126, from http://www.vatican.va/holy_father/benedict_xvi/audiences/2011/documents/hf_ben-xvi_aud_20111012_it.html. Translated by the Daughters of St. Paul.

## Chapter 19: Take the Long View

1. *Catechism of the Catholic Church,* no. 1028.

2. Patricia A. McEachern, *A Holy Life: The Writings of Saint Bernadette of Lourdes* (San Francisco: Ignatius Press, 2005), 32.

## Chapter 20: Flatter Sincerely

1. Pope Benedict XVI, "Wednesday General Audience," August 20, 2008. Last accessed January 2013 on http://www.vatican.va/holy_father/benedict_xvi/audiences/2008/documents/hf_ben-xvi_aud_20080820_en.html.

2. See Alban Butler, Donald Attwater, Herbert Thurston, *Butler's Lives of the Saints*, vol. 3 (Burns and Oates, 1956), 143.

## Chapter 22: Thanks for Sharing

1. Pope Paul VI, *On Evanglization in the Modern World, Apostolistic Exhortation, Evangelii Nuntiandi* (Boston: Pauline Books & Media, 1976), no. 14.

2. Pope John Paul II, *Mission of the Redeemer, Encyclical Letter, Redemptoris Missio* (Boston: Pauline Books & Media, 1999), Introduction, no. 2.

## Chapter 23: Don't Have a Cow

1. See Thomas G. Morrow, *Christian Courtship in an Oversexed World: A Guide for Catholics* (Huntington, IN: Our Sunday Visitor Press, 2003), 251.

## Chapter 24: Take a Trip

1. Or as we might say today, "Then do folk long to go on pilgrimage," Geoffrey Chaucer, *The Canterbury Tales*, 1380–1392. Group A, The Prologue, line 12.

2. See *The Twelve Degrees of Humility and Pride*, Saint Bernard, trans. Barton R. V. Mills (Society for Promoting Christian Knowledge, New York and Toronto: The MacMillan Co., 1929), 12.

## Chapter 25: Be a Homebody

1. *Good News Bible*, Second Edition, 1 John 4:7b.

## Chapter 26: Get a Job

1. Bishop Michael J. Saltarelli, "Holiness in the World of Work," Pastoral Statement for Labor Day 2001.

2. Ibid.

3. Ibid.

4. Blessed Mother Teresa, *The Best Gift Is Love: Meditations*, ed. Sean-Patrick Lovett (Ann Arbor, MI: Servant Publications, 1993), 113.

## Chapter 27: Lighten Your Load

1. Rick Gore, "Istanbul on Edge," *National Geographic Magazine*, vol. 202, issue 4, October 2002. Last accessed March 2013 at http://ngm. nationalgeographic.com/print/features/world/asia/turkey/ istanbul-text.

2. Sherri Dalphonse, "Love and Money," *Washingtonian Magazine*, February 1, 2000. Last accessed March 2013 at http://www. washingtonian.com/articles/people/love-money/.

3. "Mammon" is an ancient word for wealth and property.

4. See Mother Teresa and Dorothy S. Hunt, *Love, a Fruit Always in Season: Meditations from the Words of Mother Teresa* (San Francisco: Ignatius Press, 1987), 182.

5. "Simple Gifts" is a Shaker hymn written and composed in 1848 by Elder Joseph Brackett.

## Chapter 28: Kick the Habit

1. Robert J. Wicks, *Everyday Simplicity: A Practical Guide to Spiritual Growth* (Notre Dame, IN: Sorin Books, 2000), 46.

## Chapter 29: Get Help from Your Friends

1. See *Newsweek*'s "Perspectives" online column dated December 3, 2000. Last accessed at http://www.thedailybeast.com/newsweek/ 2000/12/04/perspectives.html on March 6, 2013.

2. See numbers 17 and 20 in *Devotions Upon Emergent Occasions* (1624) by John Donne.

3. Pope John Paul II, Homily for the Jubilee of Families, no. 2, October 15, 2000. Accessed June 19, 2013 at http://www.vatican.va/ holy_father/john_paul_ii/homilies/2000/documents/hf_jp-ii_ hom_20001015_families_en.html.

4. Francis of Assisi, *The Little Flowers of Saint Francis*, trans. by Sir Thomas Walker Arnold (London: J.M. Dent and Co., Aldine House, 1900), 48.

5. See Saint John Climacus, *The Ladder of Ascent*, Step 25.

6. See Robert J. Wicks, "A Wonderful Circle of Friends," *Arlington Catholic Herald*, April 19, 2001, http://www.catholicherald.com/stories/A-Wonderful-Circle-of-Friends,4675.

## Chapter 30: Count Your Blessings

1. *Orthodoxy*, 82.

## Chapter 31: Do the Dishes

1. See National Public Radio feature on "Weekly Edition" with correspondent Madeleine Brand, March 18, 2000.

2. See Ronald Rolheiser, *The Holy Longing* (New York: Doubleday, 1999), 99–101.

3. Jean-Pierre De Caussade, *Abandonment to Divine Providence: With Letters of Father de Caussade on the Practice of Self-Abandonment* (San Francisco: Ignatius Press, 2011), 106.

4. Saint Therese of Lisieux, *Story of a Soul (l'Histoire d'une Ame): The Autobiography of St. Therese of Lisieux* (London: Burns, Oates & Washbourne, 1912), edited by Rev. T. N. Taylor, trans. by Christian Classics Ethereal Library (Grand Rapids, MI, 2007), 212. Accessed April 2013 at http://www.ccel.org/ccel/therese/autobio.pdf.

5. See Martin Luther King, Jr., "Some Things We Must Do," address delivered at the 2nd Annual Institute on Nonviolence in Montgomery, AL, December 5, 1957.

## Chapter 32: Apply the Brakes

1. *Gaudium et Spes,* no. 61.

## Chapter 33: Get Your Head in the Game

1. See Nicholas King, S.J., "Saint Paul and the Olympic Games," posted on July 24, 2012, "Thinking Faith: The Online Journal of the British Jesuits, "http://www.thinkingfaith.org/articles/20120724_1.pdf.

2. See Frank Parkenham, Earl of Longford, *Pope John Paul II: An Authorized Biography* (New York: W. Morrow, 1982), 75.

3. John Paul II, "Address to the International Convention on the Theme: 'During the Time of the Jubilee: The Face and Soul of Sport,'" Saturday, October 28, 2000, posted at http://www.vatican.va/holy_father/john_paul_ii/speeches/documents/hf_jp-ii_spe_20001028_jubilsport_en.html, no. 1.

4. See "Saint Paul and the Olympic Games," referenced above.

5. Ibid.

6. See 1 Corinthians 9:24–27.

7. Nicholas King, trans., *The New Testament*, (Suffolk, UK: Kevin Mayhew, Ltd., 2004), 2 Timothy 4:7.

8. See Joseph Pronechen, "Runner Prays Across the U.S.," *National Catholic Register*, June 10, 2011. Accessed at http://www.ncregister.com/site/article/runner-prays-across-the-u.s/ on January, 2013.

9. John Paul II, "Jubilee of Sports People," October 29, 2000, at http://www.vatican.va/holy_father/john_paul_ii/homilies/documents/hf_jp-ii_hom_20001029_jubilee-sport_en.html.

## Chapter 34: Take a Hike

1. Pope Benedict XVI, "Letter to the Ecumenical Patriarch of Constantinople on the Occasion of the Seventh Symposium of the Religion, Science and the Environment Movement," September 1, 2007, http://www.vatican.va/holy_father/benedict_xvi/letters/2007/documents/hf_ben-xvi_let_20070901_symposium-environment_en.html.

2. See John Denver vocal performance of "Rocky Mountain High," written by John Denver and Mike Taylor, RCA Victor, 1972, 45 rpm.

## Chapter 35: Visit a Museum

1. Cf. Father Mariusz Casimir Koch, C.F.R., "Redeemed by Beauty—Beauty Redeemed," in *GrayFriar News*, issue 44, Summer 2011.

2. Cynthia L. Haven, "Dana Gioia Goes to Washington," *Commonweal*, November 21, 2003. http://commonwealmagazine.org/dana-gioia-goes-washington-0.

3. King James Bible, Psalm 96:9.

4. See Jem Sullivan, "Celebrating the Beauty of Faith: The Eucharist and Sacred Art" (Washington, DC: United States Conference of Catholic Bishops, 2011), http://www.usccb.org/beliefs-and-teachings/ how-we-teach/catechesis/catechetical-sunday/eucharist/upload/ catsun-2011-doc-sullivan-beauty.pdf.

5. Pope Benedict XVI, "General Audience Castel Gandolfo" on August 31, 2011, http://www.vatican.va/holy_father/benedict_xvi/ audiences/ 2011/documents/hf_ben-xvi_aud_20110831_en.html.

6. *The Confessions of St. Augustine,* Book X, ch. 27.

## Chapter 36: Bon Appétit

1. There is a widely told story, with several variations, that tells of people coming upon Teresa noisily devouring a partridge. According to the storyteller, those who came upon her were visitors, guests, novices, or fellow Carmelites. In one version, this happened while she was a guest at a monastery. In her own defense, she purportedly made a comment about their being times for eating partridge and times for porridge/penance/prayer/fasting.

## Chapter 37: Laugh Out Loud

1. Melanie Svoboda, S.N.D., *Traits of a Healthy Spirituality* (Mystic, CT: Twenty-Third Publications, 2005), 44.

2. *Love: A Fruit Always in Season; Daily Meditations by Mother Teresa*, by Mother Teresa and Dorothy S. Hunt, ed. (Ignatius Press, San Francisco, 1987), 94.

3. Saint Thomas Aquinas, *Summa Theologica,* Question 168, Article 4, Objection 3.

4. In an interview with Bayerische Rundfunk, Deutsche Welle, ZDF and Vatican Radio at Pope Benedict XVI's summer residence at Castelgandolfo on August 5, 2006, conducted in German and translated by the Vatican: http://www.dw.de/pope-benedict-xvi-we- have-a-positive-idea-to-offer/a-2129951-1.

5. Francis Thompson, *Saint Ignatius Loyola* (London: Burns and Oates, 1909), 201.

6. See John L. Allen, *All the Pope's Men: The Inside Story of How the Vatican Really Thinks* (New York: Doubleday, 2004), 16.

## Chapter 38: Throw a Party

1. See Michael O'Brien, *Father Elijah: An Apocalypse* (San Francisco: Ignatius Press, 1998), 119.

2. See Saint Augustine of Hippo, Sermon 362, 29 (PL 38:1224), "*tota actio nostra, amen et alleluia erit . . .*" ("Our entire activity will be 'Amen' and 'Alleluia.'").

3. See Ronald Rolheiser, *The Holy Longing* (New York: Doubleday, 1999), 57–59.

## Chapter 39: Sing a Song

1. Dion DiMucci and Mike Aquilina, *Dion: The Wanderer Talks Truth* (Cincinnati: Servant Books, 2011), 99.

2. Pope Benedict XVI, "Address to the Regensburg Cathedral Boys' Choir in Germany," October 22, 2005 http://www.vatican.va/holy_father/benedict_xvi/speeches/2005/october/documents/hf_ben_xvi_spe_20051022_concerto-sistina_en.html.

3. Charlene Smith and John Feister, *Thea's Song: The Life of Thea Bowman* (Maryknoll, NY: Orbis Books, 2012), 264.

4. "Sing to the Lord: Music in Divine Worship," sect. 1, par. 5 (Washington, DC: United States Conference of Catholic Bishops, issued November 14, 2007).

5. See Saint Augustine, Commentary on Psalm 73, 1: *Corpus Christianorum Latinorum* 39, 986 (*Patrologia Latina* 36, 914),

## Epilogue: Different Strokes for Different Folks

1. See United States Conference of Catholic Bishops, *United States Catholic Catechism for Adults* (Washington, DC: USCCB Publishing, 2006), 9.

2. Pope Benedict XVI, "Angelus Address for the Solemnity of the Epiphany of the Lord," January 6, 2008, http://www.vatican.va/holy_father/benedict_xvi/angelus/2008/documents/hf_ben-xvi_ang_20080106_epifania_en.html.

3. G. K. Chesterton, *The Catholic Church and Conversion* (San Francisco: Ignatius Press, 2006), 38.

4. Prosper Goepfert, *The Life of the Venerable Francis Mary Paul Libermann* (Dublin: M. H. Gill & Son, 1880), 49.

5. See Flannery O'Connor, *The Habit of Being: Letters of Flannery O'Connor*, edited by Sally Fitzgerald (New York: Farrar, Straus and Giroux, 1979), 93.

6. See Peter Hitchens, *The Rage Against God: How Atheism Led Me to Faith* (Grand Rapids, MI: Zondervan, 2010).

7. Saint Therese of Lisieux, *Story of a Soul: The Autobiography of Saint Therese of Lisieux*, Study Edition, trans. by John Clarke, O.C.D., prepared by Marc Foley, O.C.D. (Washington, DC: Institute for Carmelite Studies, 2005), 15.

# Acknowledgments

Excerpts from *Austin Farrer: The Essential Sermons*, edited by Leslie Houlden, copyright 1991 by SPCK. Used with permission.

Excerpts from *The Works of Saint Augustine: A Translation for the 21st Century*, edited by John E. Rotelle, O.S.A, and translated by L. Edmund Hill, O.P., copyright 1993 by New City Press. Used with permission.

Excerpted from *The Collected Works of St. Teresa of Avila, Volume Three* translated by Kieran Kavanaugh and Otilio Rodriguez copyright © 1980 by Washington Province of Discalced Carmelites ICS Publication 2131 Lincoln Road, N.E. Washington, DC 20002-1199 U.S.A. www.icspublications.org.

Excerpted from *Touching the Holy* by Robert J. Wicks copyright © 2007 by Ave Maria Press, PO Box 428, Notre Dame, IN 46556.

Excerpted from *Things Seen and Unseen* by Lawrence S. Cunningham copyright © 2010 by Ave Maria Press, PO Box 428, Notre Dame, IN 46556.

Excerpted from *Everyday Simplicity: A Practical Guide to Spiritual Growth* by Robert J. Wicks copyright © 2000 by Ave Maria Press, PO Box 428, Notre Dame IN 46556.

Excerpts from "Dana Gioia Goes to Washington" by Cynthia L. Haven copyright © 2003 Commonweal Foundation. Reprinted with permission. For more information, visit www.commonwealmagazine.org.

Excerpts from *Thea's Song: The Life of Thea Bowman* by Charlene Smith and John Feister copyright © 2012 by Orbis Books. Used with permission.

Excerpts from *Story of a Soul,* by Theresa of Lisieux, translated by John Clarke, O.C.D., copyright © 1975, 1976, 1996 by Washington Province of Discalced Carmelites ICS Publication 2131 Lincoln Road, N.E. Washington, DC 20002-1199 U.S.A. www.icspublications.org.

Excerpts from *Dion: The Wanderer Talks Truth* by Dion DiMucci and Mike Aquilina copyright 2011 by Servant Publications. Used with permission.

Excerpts from *The New Testament* translated by Nicholas King, ©2004 Kevin Mayhew Ltd. Reproduced by permission of Kevin Mayhew Ltd. (www.kevinmayhew.com).

Blessed Pope John Paul II's and Pope Benedict XVI's magisterium texts © by Libreria Editrice Vaticana and used with permission. All rights reserved.

# About the Author

A priest of the Archdiocese of Washington, Reverend R. Scott Hurd was baptized and raised in the Episcopal Church. He began his ordained ministry as a married Episcopal priest. In 1996, Fr. Scott entered the Catholic Church, and he was ordained a Catholic priest in 2000. He and his wife, Stephanie, live in Virginia with their three children.

Drawn from his pastoral ministry and personal experience *When Faith Feels Fragile* is Fr. Scott's third book. He has also penned the award-winning best-seller *Forgiveness: A Catholic Approach* (Pauline Books & Media 2011) and *Daily Devotions for Lent 2013* (Ave Maria Press 2012).

He has served as Executive Director of the Archdiocese of Washington's Office of the Permanent Diaconate and as Vicar General of the Personal Ordinariate of the Chair of Saint Peter.

## ALSO BY REVEREND R. SCOTT HURD

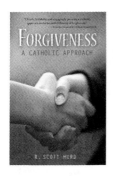

### *Forgiveness: A Catholic Approach*

Father R. Scott Hurd writes of the spiritual, psychological, physical, adn social benefits of learning how to forgive. Drawing from his pastoral experience, Hurd examines how human weakness impacts our ability to reconcile and forgive, and our capacity to trust.

Paperback      160 pages

0-8198-2691-X    $9.95

BOOKS & MEDIA

A mission of the Daughters of St. Paul

As apostles of Jesus Christ, evangelizing today's world:

We are CALLED to holiness
by God's living Word and Eucharist.

We COMMUNICATE the Gospel message
through our lives and through all
available forms of media.

We SERVE the Church
by responding to the hopes and needs
of all people with the Word of God,
in the spirit of St. Paul.

For more information visit our website: www.pauline.org.

## BOOKS & MEDIA

The Daughters of St. Paul operate book and media centers at the following addresses. Visit, call, or write the one nearest you today, or find us at www.pauline.org.

**CALIFORNIA**

| | |
|---|---|
| 3908 Sepulveda Blvd, Culver City, CA 90230 | 310-397-8676 |
| 935 Brewster Avenue, Redwood City, CA 94063 | 650-369-4230 |
| 5945 Balboa Avenue, San Diego, CA 92111 | 858-565-9181 |

**FLORIDA**

| | |
|---|---|
| 145 S.W. 107th Avenue, Miami, FL 33174 | 305-559-6715 |

**HAWAII**

| | |
|---|---|
| 1143 Bishop Street, Honolulu, HI 96813 | 808-521-2731 |
| Neighbor Islands call: | 866-521-2731 |

**ILLINOIS**

| | |
|---|---|
| 172 North Michigan Avenue, Chicago, IL 60601 | 312-346-4228 |

**LOUISIANA**

| | |
|---|---|
| 4403 Veterans Memorial Blvd, Metairie, LA 70006 | 504-887-7631 |

**MASSACHUSETTS**

| | |
|---|---|
| 885 Providence Hwy, Dedham, MA 02026 | 781-326-5385 |

**MISSOURI**

| | |
|---|---|
| 9804 Watson Road, St. Louis, MO 63126 | 314-965-3512 |

**NEW YORK**

| | |
|---|---|
| 64 W. 38th Street, New York, NY 10018 | 212-754-1110 |

**PENNSYLVANIA**

| | |
|---|---|
| Philadelphia—relocating | 215-676-9494 |

**SOUTH CAROLINA**

| | |
|---|---|
| 243 King Street, Charleston, SC 29401 | 843-577-0175 |

**VIRGINIA**

| | |
|---|---|
| 1025 King Street, Alexandria, VA 22314 | 703-549-3806 |

**CANADA**

| | |
|---|---|
| 3022 Dufferin Street, Toronto, ON M6B 3T5 | 416-781-9131 |

¡También somos su fuente para libros,
videos y música en español!